Talking Poetics

Scott Thurston has published three full-length poetry collections with Shearsman: *Hold* (2006), *Momentum* (2008) and *Internal Rhyme* (2010). He lectures at the University of Salford where he runs an MA in innovative and experimental creative writing. He edited *The Salt Companion to Geraldine Monk* (2007), co-edits the *Journal of British and Irish Innovative Poetry* (with Robert Sheppard) and is co-organiser of the Manchester-based poetry reading series, The Other Room. He lives in Liverpool.

Talking Poetics

Dialogues in Innovative Poetry

*with Karen Mac Cormack, Jennifer Moxley
Caroline Bergvall & Andrea Brady*

by

Scott Thurston

Shearsman Books

Published in the United Kingdom in 2011 by
Shearsman Books Ltd
50 Westons Hill Drive
Emersons Green
Bristol
BS16 7DF

www.shearsman.com

ISBN 978-1-84861-191-7
First Edition

Copyright © Scott Thurston, Caroline Bergvall,
Andrea Brady, Karen Mac Cormack, Jennifer Moxley, 2011

The right of Scott Thurston, Caroline Bergvall, Andrea Brady,
Karen Mac Cormack and Jennifer Moxley to be identified as the
authors of this work has been asserted by them in accordance
with the Copyrights, Designs and Patents Act of 1988.
All rights reserved.

The author wishes to gratefully acknowledge the support of the
Arts and Humanities Research Council.

Contents

Introduction 7

Karen Mac Cormack 14

Jennifer Moxley 47

Caroline Bergvall 80

Andrea Brady 103

Bibliography 144

Introduction

This book explores the poetry of Karen Mac Cormack, Jennifer Moxley, Caroline Bergvall and Andrea Brady by means of face-to-face interviews carried out between 2008 and 2009 in the UK and USA. The roots of this project lie in a series of six interviews which I conducted between 1999 and 2000 with the poets Allen Fisher, Adrian Clarke, John Wilkinson, Ira Lightman, Maggie O'Sullivan and Ulli Freer.[1] In that earlier research I was seeking to place my own poetic practice in context as well as doing critical work on the poets involved, inspired by the example of Allen Fisher in his long essay *Necessary Business* (1985), which contains excerpts from conversations with Eric Mottram and cris cheek. As both a poet and a critic, I see the interview as a kind of halfway house between full-blown academic writing and a more relaxed literary journalism, whilst also satisfying my writer's need to be in contact with my peers; sharing ideas and developing understandings that help me to orient myself in the contemporary poetic landscape. This is where the term "poetics" in the title stems from, referring to the discourse of writers reflecting on their writerly practice, following Robert Sheppard's definitions in his essay 'The Necessity of Poetics'.[2]

In the interviews that comprise this book I wanted to discover what were the most important creative issues facing these poets. I was curious about their views on innovation, on literary theory and literary history, on teaching, politics, gender, aesthetics, performance, language and so on. I also wanted to get closer to understanding the origins, intentions, and meanings of specific examples of their work from across their respective oeuvres. My approach was informed in part by my ongoing interest in the relationship between what Barrett Watten calls *method* and *technique* in writing—which I paraphrase as distinguishing between the part of the writing that is to do with *why* it is made (method) and the part which is to do with *how* it is made (technique).[3] I am fascinated by the subtle

---

[1] Published in issues of the Austrian journal *Poetry Salzburg Review* between 2002 and 2006.

[2] See Robert Sheppard, 'The Necessity of Poetics' (2000). Viewable at: http://www.pores.bbk.ac.uk/1/Robert%20Sheppard,%20'The%20Necessity%20of%20Poetics'.htm

[3] See the interviews with Karen Mac Cormack and Jennifer Moxley. I have also considered these terms in 'If Poetry is Private Language Aspiring to be Public, How Should One Write?' in *Poetry and Public Language*, ed. by Anthony Caleshu and Tony Lopez, (Exeter: Shearsman Books, 2007) pp. 263–269 and 'Audience and Representation: Method and Technique', *The Paper* 9 (2007), 39–53 as well as in my Ph.D. thesis entitled *Rescale: Method and Technique in Contemporary British Linguistically Innovative Poetry and Poetics* (University of Lancaster, 2002).

relationships between these aspects as they play out across a body of writing. To the extent that they might be hard to separate, and may indeed be a somewhat artificial distinction,[4] I consider them as the opposite ends of a scale of attention that runs from the macro level of method down to the micro level of technique. Throughout these conversations this scale is reflected in the movement between general discussions of poetics and close readings of actual poems.

Why did I choose these particular poets? In Karen Mac Cormack's case, I was particularly drawn to her remarkable project *Implexures* (1993–2007), which I first became aware of when I was a participant in a webcast of a poetry reading that Mac Cormack and Allen Fisher gave at the Kelly Writer's House in Philadelphia in October 2001 as part of the Philly Talks series.[5] I then followed the project's development in various published extracts. As it turned out, the opening part of the interview with Mac Cormack took place in London in 2008 the day after the British launch of the first complete edition of *Implexures* at Birkbeck College, University of London. In the interview, Mac Cormack describes *Implexures* as her "transhistorical polybiography". This complex term refers to the origins of the project as a response to a family biography published in the 1950s by her great Aunt, the novelist Susan Hicks Beach. This is augmented with letters to and from Mac Cormack's parents and an impressive range of literary, philosophical, scientific and historical material from various periods: covering particle physics and postmodern architecture alongside the semiotics of the Japanese fan and readings of Aphra Behn. My own fascination with *Implexures* arose from its daring combinations of diverse materials, and its interest in presenting information within the context of an enquiry into time and identity—the kind of enquiry that was driving my own creative projects at the time, in my books *Momentum* and *Internal Rhyme*.[6]

---

[4] Such as that between form and content—perhaps permanently undone by Charles Olson's famous adoption of Robert Creeley's statement that "form is never more than an extension of content", in Charles Olson, 'Projective Verse' (1950), in Donald Allen and Warren Tallman, eds., *The Poetics of the New American Poetry* (New York: Grove Press Inc., 1973), pp. 147-84, p. 148.
[5] The Phillytalks event is available on the Penn Sound website at: http://www.writing.upenn.edu/pennsound/phillytalks/Philly-Talks-Episode19.html. The pre-event correspondence between Mac Cormack and Fisher can be viewed at: http://slought.org/files/downloads/domains/phillytalks/pdf/pt19.pdf
[6] Scott Thurston, *Momentum* (Exeter: Shearsman Books, 2008), *Internal Rhyme* (Exeter: Shearsman Books, 2010).

Introduction

Jennifer Moxley's autobiography *The Middle Room* (Subpress, 2007) represented a very different approach to writing about identity. A kind of *biographia literaria*, the memoir describes her early poetic career growing up in San Diego, attending the University of California at San Diego (UCSD), and moving to Providence with her partner Steve Evans shortly before the death of her mother. Moxley attended UCSD at the time various prominent figures in the Language Poetry movement were teaching or visiting there, such as Stephen Rodefer, Rae Armantrout, Michael Davidson and Fanny Howe, and her memoir sketches intimate portraits of these figures, whilst also capturing the influence of their work on a younger writer. I found *The Middle Room* a fascinating enterprise because of its more direct exploration of the autobiographical themes otherwise present in Moxley's poetry. Seeing the transfer of this kind of activity between poetry and prose suggested a possible mode for extending the range of my own autobiographically-driven poetry: a parallel means of transforming the material of experience. In this sense my interest in Moxley was related to Mac Cormack's albeit very different approach to autobiographical material.

In terms of the technical challenges of wanting to extend the range of my own poetic production, Caroline Bergvall's work came into view as one of the most plural practices in contemporary writing. Bergvall works across poetry, visual art, installations and performances and I wanted to try to understand what made this diversity possible, and what gave it its integrity. Much to my surprise, in the course of interviewing Bergvall I found her also to be engaged in autobiographical writing in two projects entitled *Cropper* and *Plessjør*, and, as our dialogue developed, I came to see the origins of her diverse practice in her pluri-lingual and cross-cultural identity. Bergvall was born in Norway and brought up in France before moving to the UK, and speaks Norwegian, French and English. This complex background very much informs her creative practice, and the fact that she was also exploring this inheritance through autobiographical as well as multi-media modes was an important discovery for me in suggesting further possible lines of development for my own writing.

The role of Andrea Brady's work in the project was to provide a space for an ongoing thinking-through of the function and status of organised political critique in contemporary poetry in general, with a view to developing it in my own work in particular. Brady's hypertext poem *Tracking Wildfire* was an entry point here (although political concerns are apparent across her writing) in its response to the history of incendiary devices in warfare: linking the mystery of the ancient weapon of Greek fire—an early form of napalm—to the use of white phosphorous in the United States' assault on Fallujah in April 2004 during the Iraq War. I wanted to understand something more about Brady's commitment to using lyric and other poetic forms to operate critiques of the foreign policy of Western governments and the various forms of consumer capitalism in the UK and elsewhere. As it was, another of the big surprises of the project was finding out that Brady was also engaged in a new series of poems about motherhood and child development, following the birth of her daughter Ayla. Whilst not exactly autobiographical, I felt that this new work by Brady in some way also presented an enquiry into the formation of identity which put it in company with the other poets and with my own interests.

Aside from these quite personal modes of engagement, another important question driving this project was that of the use and value of the term *innovative* in relation to the practices of the poets chosen. This in a sense was still a personal question, connected to my own creative background and ongoing commitments as a poet, but it is also an issue which is being debated more widely in British poetry and academia. Innovation is certainly a fraught concept when used in relation to cultural practices, but its adjectival use in terms such as *formally innovative poetry*, or *Linguistically Innovative Poetry*, demonstrates its history of being used to refer to British and Irish poetry which has otherwise been described as avant-garde, experimental, neo-modernist, non-mainstream, post-avant, postmodernist, and as constituting a "parallel tradition".[7] I have argued in a piece of critical writing, following Ric Caddel and Peter Quartermain's argument in the introduction to their anthology *Other: British and Irish Poetry since 1970* (1998), that it is as important to recognise the commitment of innovative poetries to a literary-historical tradition of dissent (which might include such writers as Blake or Shelley, for example) as their commitment to innovation in poetic form or what Caddel and Quartermain call a "poetics of displacement".[8] As it was, in the interviews I broached the theme of innovation in various ways—enquiring of Mac

---

[7] A term used by poet-publisher Ken Edwards in his article 'The Two Poetries'. *Angelaki* 3.1 (April 2000): 25–36.
[8] See Richard Caddel and Peter Quartermain, eds., *Other: British and Irish Poetry since 1970* (Hanover and London: Wesleyan University Press, 1998), p. xx. See also Scott Thurston, 'Innovative Poetry in Britain Today', *Revista Canaria de Estudios Ingleses* 60 (April, 2010), 15–30.

Cormack why it was important, of Bergvall what she saw as the key issues facing innovative poets, of Moxley what was the function of innovation in her work and in contemporary writing, and of Brady simply what she made of the term. Whilst I don't want to pre-empt their responses here, asking the question in these various ways elicited a rich range of responses which displayed quite striking continuities and discontinuities.

There were of course many other areas of enquiry explored in these conversations which are too numerous to itemise here, and which to do so would start to undermine the integrity of these dialogues as discursive and analytical texts in their own right. Instead it is hoped that readers of these interviews will enjoy drawing out their own connections between the poets and, at the same time, find fuel for their own creative speculations and further explorations of the extraordinary work of these writers. To this purpose the interviews are footnoted and there are extensive bibliographies provided for each poet.

In terms of the project's effect on my own creative development, this is very much an ongoing process. Studying the work of these poets has led me to experiment with using more directly autobiographical material and more formally diverse structures in my writing, but perhaps one of the most significant outcomes has been a greater awareness of the importance of style in understanding poetry. Barrett Watten defines style as a "determinate pattern of differences" leading to "an autonomous idiosyncratic set of values"[9] and, although his definition ultimately carries a more oppositional charge, it has been in the transitions from my total immersion in the work of one poet to the next that the patterns of each writer's "gestural repertoire"[10] became vividly apparent. It may be difficult to make an apprehension of a poet's style available to critical analysis. To some extent it must simply be accepted as the means by which their poetry comes to us, and something which we may come to be more or less aware of, perhaps not unlike the rhythm of someone's walk. However, style is not an absolute value behind a writer's production. Where this heightened awareness of style has become useful to me is in creating the possibility of expanding my repertoire by more fully grasping the lineaments of my "default" approach to writing, so that I might start to move beyond it.

---

[9] Barrett Watten, *Total Syntax* (Carbondale and Edwardsville: Southern Illinois University Press, 1985), p. 32.
[10] A term used by John Wilkinson in his essay 'Counterfactual Prynne: An Approach to *Not-You*,' *Parataxis: Modernism and Modern Writing*, no. 8/9 (1996), 190–202, 195.

Before bringing this introduction to a conclusion, it seems worth reflecting on the nature of the medium of the interview itself, beyond my characterisation of it above as a "halfway house" between academic writing and journalism. The interview's unpredictability and reflexive nature makes it a mercurial form ideally suited to the discussion of creativity, yet it also has its opacities, its limitations, its failing to get to the truth which is symptomatic of much human communication. In a project of this kind however, there is also the paradox of tying down this mercuriality in prose—tidying it up, rewriting, restructuring, annotating—that suggests almost a kind of violence visited on the spoken text by the time it reaches the reader. Transcribing these interviews was an extraordinarily labour-intensive task. Having recorded around fourteen hours of conversation, the transcription process alone took over a hundred hours. There then followed two further revisions before the text was returned to the interviewee to make their own changes, following which a further revision would take place. This meticulous concentration on turning the mercury of speech into the lead of type was a sort of alchemy of meditation and reflection. As much as I was tempted at times to hand over the task to an audio typist, I felt that I would be missing out on the unique opportunity of re-living these ungraspable moments—tiny shifts, overtones, even background interventions—that, as I edited them out, or let them pass by unacknowledged, conveyed something of the human dimension of the contact: a mood passing through, a slight challenge received well or less well, a misconstrual, distraction, warmth and humour.

Although an earlier plan for this project envisaged accompanying chapters of critical writing on each poet, my decision instead to simply present the interviews by themselves reflects a hopeful belief in their intrinsic interest as collaborative works of poetics, that is, as conversations oriented around the creative process and its productions. Such an approach allows the poems and other writings to still have their day, ultimately uncorralled by their authors' apparent intentions for them. Because, as all writers know, writings have their own secret life which escapes the writer, which eludes her or him, and without which the whole endless, sacrificial labour of writing would be worthless.

Scott Thurston

Talking Poetics

Karen Mac Cormack

This interview was conducted in Bloomsbury, Central London on 13 June 2008 and in Buffalo, New York on 7 and 8 April 2009.

Scott Thurston: Why is innovation in creative practice important?

Karen Mac Cormack: Because without it, tradition would rule supreme as it does in most disciplines. If one doesn't seek to be contemporary with one's own time then what does it mean to write poetry in 2008? The answer would be very different if that question were posed in 1908 or 1608: the issues that we face are both the same and utterly different. So how does innovative writing engage with these concerns? Well, is the sonnet form, for example, vital to us in our understanding of the world? I would say "yes", but if there aren't as many sonnets being written now, there's a reason for that. And language, especially English, changes. New words come into being, new ways of employing words. For example, now we have everything being turned into verbs. But truly do we want to keep reading the same kinds of poetry? Yes, we want to visit them, but one also has to think in terms of what other disciplines bring to poetry. For me it's unthinkable not to consider *Finnegans Wake* a great gift to poetry. And I've certainly talked enough about Djuna Barnes' *Nightwood* in other interviews and contexts.

ST: To what extent do you see a relationship between women's creativity and innovation, given your inclusion in anthologies like *Out of Everywhere* and in the context of projects like *How2*?

KMC: I don't think of it in those terms very often. If I'm excited by a text, it really doesn't matter to me as to the gender of the writer. Certainly when I find a work (created by a woman) that I'm inspired by or excited by, I'm happy, but if anything there aren't as many women innovative writers, at least not writing in English, as there are men. I'm not sure that matters. My inclusion in various anthologies came rather late. The feminists when I was young weren't interested in my work because it wasn't essentialist enough. I was not encouraged by the elder women poets who I met, rather it was the men who were encouraging me. Am I a feminist? Yes. Do I make a point of bringing this to everyone's attention most of the time the way some other writers do? No. I'm not sure if that really answers the question.

I think that poetry would be bereft without the work of Mina Loy. My relationship to Stein's writings has changed quite a bit over the years. I used to think that Stein was a remarkable innovator, but increasingly as I read these books on shorthand techniques dating from the late nineteenth century through the nineteen forties, I wonder if Stein had access to them. This is my new thinking—was she reading these things? Because the sentences that are in them and the way they are put together, they're not meant to be read as a continuous narrative, but there is something even in the diction if you read them aloud. I read one brief passage to Steve (McCaffery) and asked him whose work it reminded him of, to which he replied "Stein". There's research to be done.

ST: That's intriguing.

KMC: So what do we mean by innovation?!

ST: Barrett Watten views the poem as "a material condensation of the social logics that created it"[1] and he wants poetry to show a connection to the conditions of its own production.

KMC: That's like putting the hem on the outside of a garment.

ST: Yes, but it also seems to me exactly like what you've just described in this possible relationship between Stein and the strange texts you get in these typing manuals—it would be an example of how there's a larger cultural logic surrounding Stein's texts. Watten called it "total syntax"— that there's a syntax of the world and a syntax of the work and the extent to which they correspond or engage with each other produces a certain kind of poetry.[2] I thought this was quite a good way of thinking about how books of yours like *Fit to Print*, *At Issue* and *Vanity Release* engage with these discourses of different media like magazines and newspapers and typing manuals.

---

[1] See Barrett Watten, 'The Expanded Object of the Poetic Field' in *Poetry and Public Language*, ed. by Tony Lopez and Anthony Caleshu (Exeter: Shearsman Books, 2007), p. 285. See also Watten's *The Constructivist Moment: From Material Text to Cultural Poetics* (Middletown, CT: Wesleyan University Press, 2003).

[2] In his essay 'Total Syntax: The Work in the World', Watten argues that the syntax of a work of art, in any medium, has both "intrinsic" and "extrinsic" dimensions and proposes a "more total syntax for the statement that is the work of art": "the interior and exterior syntax are not separate; rapidly they merge in the vast array of possibilities". Barrett Watten, *Total Syntax* (Carbondale and Edwardsville: Southern Illinois University Press, 1985), p. 68.

KMC: But in those texts I wanted to take something out of one context and put it another in order to produce something non-habitual. When you read a magazine such as *Vogue*, the language in it isn't all that different to the language in a newspaper, occasionally you'll get some buzzwords and fashion terms, but it's not as specialized as medical discourse, or mathematical, or technical. To remove groupings of words and to reinvent them into a poem, I'm not sure that's so different really. I mean are we any more aware of the materiality of language by breaking things down to phonemes or even letters? All the written words are comprised from letters in the alphabet. If you want to show the workings of our particular alphabet, what are you going to do, take it back to the Sumerian? Show the development of how various alphabets came into being? That might be interesting, some of the time—I don't know if I would want to focus on that all of the time.

ST: So in a sense it's just finding language material where it happens to be, rather than necessarily making a conscious argument between different kinds of discourse? But that's still part of it, isn't it? You were saying about turning it into something unfamiliar. Do you want to have some kind of critical relationship to those discourses?

KMC: Very much so. I think it's too easy for people to become accustomed to how something is presented to them, whether that's information on the news, say on television, or radio, or in the case of the newspaper, in print. When I began *Fit to Print* it was as a response to (being absolutely furious with) the spelling mistakes, line and word breaks in print journalism. I thought that if people could negotiate these in a newspaper and not question or complain about them, yet still say to me "I don't read poetry because it's too difficult" then I wondered what would happen if you presented a poem in a form which was immediately recognizable—columns for example—and work with the vocabulary that you find in the newspaper, everyday life, signage, and present it to them to see where that might go. Actually what Alan Halsey and I really wanted to do was to have *Fit to Print* not as a book but as a tabloid. However, Coach House Press for all their innovation, experimentation—and yes the two are different—over the years, baulked at that. They said, "how can we sell it as a book? We can't!" So, yes, if you take anything out of context what happens?

ST: In *At Issue* you also include poems which aren't derived from magazines and I wonder if you can say a bit more about why that was important—was it just to create more variety in the book or was there a formal argument that you wanted to posit?

KMC: I wanted to combine the two in part to show their similarities and their differences. I must say I tend to break out of whatever formal constraint I set myself and I find following anything too rigidly produces something that becomes recognizable in and of itself, if it's a strategy. When I read other people's work where you can see the formal constraint, it's all set out very neatly, and then there are variations on a theme, I find myself asking if you let yourself step out of that for a minute, then what might happen? What else could you write, how would that inform the formal constraint, what would you then do? It seems to me that in terms of innovative writing, one writes through things, one deals with certain issues, one creates new definitions, new rules maybe, as long as they work for a given project, and then one takes them apart again and goes on. Nothing is static, not even this table. All those molecules! Even if we think the table is solid, it isn't really.

ST: That reminds me of Allen Fisher's approach to procedure and process, he's exactly happy to break it mid-way or undo it, not to be too beholden to a system, even if it's one of his own devising.

KMC: I think his work in particular focuses on surprising people: what would happen if I do this now? I love reading Allen Fisher's work for that reason. I love listening to him read it because something unexpected happens all the time.

ST: I wanted to ask you about *Implexures*, as a total project and also how it got built. The material in it is extraordinarily diverse—how does it relate, if at all, to more normative practices of biographical and autobiographical writing?

KMC: There is a family biography written by my great-great aunt, Susan Hicks Beach, *The Yesterdays Behind the Door*,[3] in which she traces her grandfather Samuel's line, the Christians from the Isle of Man, and that of her grandmother Anne (née Gregorie), his wife. As I wrote in *Implexures*,

---

[3] Published by Liverpool University Press in 1956.

"the family goes in all directions"—there's no such thing as a family tree, there are many trees, because all of a sudden "*it*" burgeons into so many threads the further back one goes. How to navigate all of this? Well, now there are databases for such things but not when she wrote that book. (I don't know how many years it was in the works.) It was published in the year of my birth and I grew up reading it at intervals. At first I wasn't all that interested. (I never met her as she died in 1958.) Later on, in September of 1993—Steve and I were living in Kingston, Ontario—I re-read it again, realizing this was how she engaged with the notion of family. I asked myself what I could do to provide a riposte to this work, *and* to continue what she began, but to do so by encouraging poetic forces to shape the prose. Beyond that, I wanted to take the idea of autobiography and to put it firmly in the context of polybiography. Because one does not live one's life in a vacuum and how one engages with everyone who comes into one's life is very important. So how is all of this reflected in a polybiography?—with birth. That part would be autobiographical, I will introduce myself into the world. The poetry was never far from the surface, the poetry comes very much in and out and in... Someone else who just finished reading it in its entirety, said to me that he found it symphonic, which surprised me. I'm still thinking about that.

ST: Why did it surprise you?

KMC: Much as I love and appreciate music, I don't play any instruments, I've never studied music. He's a musician, a composer. Perhaps I'm on to something that I don't really understand or perhaps that's his response because of what he does. I wanted to include all the research that I was engaged in and I was reading in vastly different areas. *Implexures* did not come to me as a fully formed idea, all I knew was that I wanted to respond (creatively) to this work that my great-great aunt published. There was a lot of editing. It was written in two notebooks. My other writing meant that I published six books between 1993 and 2007 when I finished it (including *Implexures Volume One* in 2003) so it wasn't as if I worked on it exclusively. I tend to be involved in more than one project at a time. But *Implexures* was with me longer than anything else I've ever worked on. Thirteen and a half years is a long time. And, as Alan Halsey said, it's both not a big book and it is a big book because there's a lot in it. There's a lot of information in *Implexures*.

ST: In *Implexures* you have these units that you're working with, quite a lot of them are called 'Historical Letters,' and they're often given an epigraph. Then there are materials distinguished by italics, which I noticed that you don't read in performance.

KMC: It doesn't work as well. Perhaps if somebody else were to read those, perhaps if another voice were added, it would work. When one reads it aloud how does one convey the italics? It's easy to do it on the page because you just change the font. It's about the register.

ST: Do we learn who wrote the letters? Does it matter?

KMC: I identified some of them but not many. One of the things I decided to do was to re-read in its entirety the correspondence between my paternal grandparents and my parents and myself, and myself and my parents. They saved everything, boxes and more boxes of handwritten correspondence, so I read all of it and decided to include some of this material but how to introduce it? I left home when I was seventeen, travelled extensively and lived in many different countries. We wrote letters regularly and we all kept them (including theirs to me). So, in the course of re-reading my grandparents' letters I thought, oh well, I'd better read my own, since they're here. That was a very odd experience, to read what was written when I was seventeen, eighteen years old through my twenties, even into my early thirties.

Well, what to do? Make it obvious; "1980", "1976"? No, dispense with the century, just give decade and the month, that way the reader would not know (initially) which century these were from. Of course, it does become clear, from references in the letters from my grandparents: World War One for example. But again, it was not a matter of this simply being my autobiography, because my life is informed by these other people who are very important to me. So I wanted it to be initially ambiguous and eventually recognisable. How does the reader negotiate this? Is it important to know who wrote the letters? I'm not sure. A student of mine brought it to my attention that somebody has posted information about me on Wikipedia. I don't know who produced it but the reference to *Implexures* is very interesting. To paraphrase: is it all fictional or is this truly a combination of autobiography along with other things? No-one knows for sure.[4]

---

[4] The relevant part of the Wikipedia entry reads: "The prose pieces in the recent project *Implexures* are somewhat untypical in their use of biographical and autobiographical materials, especially a series of letters written from a

ST: Did that surprise you?

KMC: It surprised me that somebody actually thought that it was a book of fiction! I guess I'm too close to it. When I really step back it's a huge giant step that I have to take. I guess if I walked into a bookstore and picked up a copy I might think that it was a creation. But I still find it odd, it's difficult for me to come to terms with that.

ST: Is polybiography a term you came up with?

KMC: No, Steve McCaffery did. We were trying for an alternative to "autobiography" and he thought "polybiography" a more accurate definition of the work. I agree! There was another application of polybiography before Steve but it was in a different context.[5] So, I refer to *Implexures* as my trans-historic polybiography. There's the notion of time and what happens when you fold time in on itself or forward and back on itself and that really is, if anything, an obsession throughout. The historical letters came about when I'd been reading Derrida and then there was the Susan Hicks Beach and I thought well, yes, let's somehow put these two in conversation. And then all these other instances would occur. Last night, when I read it backwards,[6] which I'd never done before, I realized that for me, *Implexures* is in the order it's in for a reason. But there's no reason why somebody else couldn't take it apart and put it together again in a very different way, not in the order in which it is presented.

ST: I was enjoying doing just that this morning! I was flicking through the new book to find what you read last night and I was getting distracted by things that leapt out at me and by looking back over something I'd already read in the other edition and finding it different in the new presentation. But I can also see how it's important to recognize that the structure does have a particular order. When you were actually building one of these historical letters, how did they come about? Was it always the

---

variety of Mediterranean locations by an unnamed female traveller (possibly to be identified with the author, possibly not)". http://en.wikipedia.org/wiki/Karen_Mac_Cormack, accessed 16 February 2009.

[5] In John Hall's very useful essay on *Implexures*, he discusses the use of the term polybiography in the context of a "participatory method devised for compiling a history of medical sonography through the medium of an internet discussion list". See John Hall, 'Karen Mac Cormack's *Implexures*: An Implicated Reading' in Nate Dorward, ed., *Antiphonies: Essays on Women's Experimental Poetries in Canada* (Toronto: The Gig, 2008), pp. 227–247, p. 227.

[6] Mac Cormack had performed alongside Steve McCaffery the night before the interview at Birkbeck College, University of London (12 June 2008).

same approach? Did you work across a number simultaneously?

KMC: The first one was reading Derrida and the fact that Beach capitalized "difference". I read a lot of Aphra Behn in the early nineties and it really did seem as if Charles Bernstein and Aphra Behn could have been conversing. The idea of the fan and time, that fascinated me; what if we could do something with time the way a fan does something with surfaces and space?

ST: So literally folding it back on itself?

KMC: Or forward into itself. It works both ways. The poem '*On Reading an Inland Ferry*'[7] originated in the vocabulary found in the novel of the same name by Susan Hicks Beach. She's best known for her *Cardinal of the Medici*,[8] ostensibly a novel but usually considered historical biography. I didn't deliberately read one thing and seek its counterpart or its response in another. I made notes of things that I found interesting and I would go through these and slowly but surely they would fit together, some of them. I experimented quite a bit by moving text around: when to make an episode occur within the information being provided in a given section? It was time-consuming. For me it was an ambitious structure to embark on. Keeping all the balls in the air proved to be quite the challenge. Sometimes I would find myself wondering where I was going to introduce information on a given subject and I would sometimes do so "too soon" because I was worried that I would lose track of it somehow … hence the editing and re-editing. I learned to relax and to realize it doesn't matter how long it takes to do this. The only reason that "volume one" was published in 2003 was because many people were asking: "When are you going to finish this, when are you going to publish it?" and I reached a stage where I considered there to be a logical break of what could be termed "volume one", namely, after section nineteen.

Then the pressure mounted to produce "volume two". Meanwhile volume one went out of print (nearly) so the decision was made to publish the "complete edition".

ST: I'm delighted it's here. I think it's an important book.

KMC: I don't know how important it is to know its method of composition.

---

[7] See Karen Mac Cormack, *Implexures* (Tucson, AZ, and Sheffield: Chax Press and West House Books, 2008), pp. 47–49.
[8] Published by Cambridge University Press in 1937.

I suppose I'm leaving things out.

ST: I'm not sure how helpful it is either. But I find the book's approach to structure very liberating. For me its power lies in how it allows me to follow the way your thought moves and yet also to engage deeply with different kinds of material. I love the way in which you treat what I take to be your own experience—the anecdotes, accounts of dreams—and then you swerve into something very different. I'm asking a sort of writerly question which I think does nothing more than extend the permission. The poem answers it, almost answers it, itself in what I take to be descriptions or analyses of its own on-going processes.

KMC: There is another aspect vis à vis *Implexures*, which I didn't realize until "volume one" was included on a course at the State University of Maine (Orono) by Carla Billitteri in the spring of 2004. (I was invited by Steve Evans, Carla and Jennifer Moxley to read there that spring). I met with Carla's students who provided written responses and it was a focused experience for all concerned, during which I realized that subconsciously I had wanted to write a poetic work that would be read by people who don't usually read and listen to poetry. For me it was a wonderful realization.

ST: I think that's part of what I find so liberating about it: there's almost nothing that can't go into a structure like that. That's not to say that there isn't scrupulous decision-making going on, but the breadth of what you're able to combine is thrilling, and a real incentive for creativity: to make those kinds of connections and to view time in a way that is much more complex than usually conceived of. Is Proust relevant to your thinking about time?

KMC: I read *Remembrance of Things Past* (i.e. the English translation) when I was in my late twenties. My first attempt to read it was when I was 15 or 16—that wasn't the right time for me!—I managed the first thirty pages and I thought if it takes thirty pages for the little boy to go to sleep then what on earth is going to be discussed in even greater detail in the coming hundreds of pages?! That's when I read *Nightwood* though. Proust's treatment of time is very much his own, I won't say there's an influence. His extended sentences and meditations gave me a sense of what was possible within writing. A work that was far more influential was Robert Musil's *The Man Without Qualities*. I've read both the Picador translation, which was published in the 1970s and more recently I read the Knopf/

Karen Mac Cormack

Borzoi edition when it came out in 2000 (both are incomplete as Musil died before finishing the project). I would argue that it's more a book of philosophy than anything else, it just happens to take the form of a novel. But it proved a revelation to me. And then I read Musil's notebooks and some of the ideas about creating works involving temporal shifts I found liberating myself.

ST: Deleuze seems to be quite an important presence in your work in a number of different contexts.

KMC: Deleuze provided his insights at the right moment for me in many instances and his work with Guattari I consider ongoingly rewarding. Proust's focus on time was so much in the past that there wasn't enough embracing of the present or the future. I'm interested in where we are at the moment thinking about notions of time, such as the idea that there could be many more dimensions than we are aware of, curled up one within another. I've read a lot about string theory: I am fascinated by each new development, each new discovery. The very fact that scientists managed to teleport atoms recently, all of a sudden made *Star Trek* seem less far-fetched. That was exciting. It was a very short article saying, basically, well, yes, it's been proven that it can be done but don't start thinking "beam me up Scotty" just yet with human beings. But if one can't travel through time, then what's the closest experience one can have to that? I think we only really get that in dreams, or in extraordinary circumstances where something will trigger a memory. Or intuition can sometimes have that temporal foresight, if you will. You sense that something is going to happen and then it does. It's as if part of your psyche is a few steps ahead, closer to the future than the present.

ST: Yes, I find those kinds of experiences fascinating too. I want to ask you about *The Tongue Moves Talk* (1997). In two online interviews you mention the "social concept of the carrier" in connection with that book[9]. My understanding of a carrier is a social entity which carries a technique into society. I was wondering if you could say something about how the book illustrates that notion? I was particularly interested in the poem 'At

---

[9] Antoine Cazé, 'An Interview with Karen Mac Cormack and Steve McCaffery' in *Sources*, no. 8 (Spring 2000), 28–47. Viewable at: http://www.paradigme.com/sources/SOURCES-PDF/Pages%20de%20Sources08-1-5.pdf; Stephen Cain, 'Interview with Karen Mac Cormack' in *Queen Street Quarterly*, vol. 3, no. 4 (Winter 2000), 53–61. Viewable at: http://epc.buffalo.edu/authors/maccormack/interview.html

Issue' which appears in a partly revised version in *At Issue* (2001).

KMC: Again, overlapping projects. Yes, language as a carrier of meaning, woman as carrier of the species, disease as a carrier of menace, sometimes death. How do these notions impact on language and what do we do with language when it isn't a carrier of information or instantaneous meaning, when we complicate it by making it poetry that isn't necessarily easily understood upon first reading? Some of those poems are quite dark. Some of them describe things that are happening in the world as I know it in a critical way: human injustice to other human beings, certain symptoms of society going very much awry, social conditions unfortunate at best and reprehensible.

Do the poems evoke this? I hope so. I don't address specifically woman as carrier of the species, but I was thinking about that as part of the overall concept. Sometimes women are perceived only as carriers: their worth in certain societies is to provide a son, and if a daughter, to be dealt with accordingly. When is woman not a carrier? What does it mean for a woman to be a poet and to eschew the option of being a carrier of the species? So these were concerns that were in the air and certainly found their way into those poems. I was thinking about how language shapes us as much as we think we shape language.

ST: In connection with that point about language, the book closes with this extraordinary poem 'Resex'. I wonder if you could say a bit about how that was written? It traverses many different kinds of discourses.

KMC: I was reading the dictionary, many dictionaries, dictionaries are wonderful! Dictionaries of etymology, dictionaries of slang. When I happened upon "resex" and its meaning—"the stub left on a pruned branch"—I pondered. Pruning affects both the branch and the tree. When one sees "resex" for the first time, one's first thought isn't of stubs on pruned branches (or at least it wasn't mine). But when applied to language and how one creates new words and how neologisms form and what that does to the words that gave part of their meaning to create a new one, what resulted was this poem, which, as I recall, was written over a period of time and required considerable editing. (Its ending "disentangled fact vernacular" is my response to the meaning of "resex".)

Many of my poems are either responses to, or meditations on, meaning being taken out of context. The title 'I'm Big On Ladders', can mean all sorts of things. And the way meanings change over time was one reason I became so fascinated with slang. Perhaps you know this already, but in Victorian England, "gay" meant a young female prostitute and it was only in the first two decades of the twentieth century that it became a code for homosexual. But we don't understand "gay" in the sense of a young female prostitute anymore. And "gay" as in "to be happy", I don't think anybody refers to that these days, do they? So, why is it that these things happen, and why is it that they only happen to some meanings of words and some words themselves and not others?

ST: What other kinds of writing interest you?

KMC: I'm interested in letters writers have written to one another. I remember in particular reading Virginia Woolf's correspondence with Vita Sackville-West and how "alive" those letters were. That became important to me as something to do, to write well. I don't "dash off" letters and actually most of the time I treat e-mail as a replacement for letter-writing. Often I'll sit down, compose a draft, consider what I want to convey and how I want to express myself, and then I will cut and paste and eventually the correspondence is printed out. I do think it's important to know how to write in different forms and what it means to explore something that you don't do well (initially), until you become adept at it, or overcome whatever difficulties. I know that this expanded and gave greater depth to my own work.

ST: Where do you think you'll go next after completing *Implexures*?

KMC: There is life after *Implexures*! I've been working on what I call my non project-related poems. However, there is a new project with the working title of *Machicolated Conversations*. "Machicolated" is an architectural term meaning "to furnish with openings (as in a parapet)" although I'm less interested in the military association of the openings affording defence, i.e. "dropping stones etc. on assailants". My inclination is to see what happens by allowing the unanticipated in through the openings. I'm working on the second poem; the first one is being published in the journal *New American Writing*. I'm revising and working on my essays, which I'm now being pestered about publishing!

ST: Going back a bit to time and memory, I was interested in how the architectural element in *Implexures* is linked to the loci of mnemonics.

KMC: Mary Carruthers![10] Yes, that figures prominently in terms of memory. How memory becomes distorted, how accurate one's memory is, ways of thinking about memory, improving memory. What became increasingly compelling for me, especially in reading Carruthers, was discovering that in medieval times it was considered an ethical responsibility to write and comment upon what you had been reading. If you could add to this knowledge-base, then it was your duty to do so, so that others might benefit. In thinking about why people write today, how often is it that someone says, "I find it my ethical responsibility to do what I can to contribute to whatever tradition or non-tradition I choose to"? You don't hear that very often. Is this a good thing? I don't know. It's an observed fact. Many people when asked why they write reply "because I want to". That doesn't get you very far in terms of why is it important to write, what you hope for in a reader. The notion of the model reader is an encouraging one I suppose. But what do you do if someone reads your work and really doesn't know what to do with it? Then what happens? Should you even be thinking about that?

ST: You spoke earlier about *Implexures* as something to be read by those who don't normally relate to poetry and this feels consciously ethical to me.

KMC: Yes, absolutely. Getting back to architecture, I've always been interested in it but not for the same reasons. When the architect Tom Emerson told me what he thought my poetry was doing in architectural terms (when I met him at the CCCP[11] in Cambridge, England in 1997) I really started paying attention to architecture because he "opened" it for me in terms of how poetry could engage with architectural environments.

At that time I read Bernard Cache's *Earth Moves* (in translation).[12] This was his dissertation and I think he was the only architect who worked with Deleuze, who was the thesis supervisor, as I recall. Hence the "fold" in architecture as a way of thinking about form became for me a strategy for *Implexures* and other writings.

---

[10] Carruthers' books include: *The Medieval Craft of Memory: An Anthology of Texts and Pictures* (with J. M. Ziolkowski) (Philadelphia: University of Pennsylvania Press, 2002); *The Craft of Thought: Meditation, Rhetoric and the Making of Images: 400–1200* (Cambridge University Press, 1998) and *The Book of Memory: A Study of Memory in Medieval Culture* (Cambridge: Cambridge University Press, 1990).
[11] The Cambridge Conference of Contemporary Poetry.
[12] See footnote 28.

ST: Is it the fold in the fan as well? [**KMC**: Yes.] So, it's not so much the spacial analogies of memory that might be considered architectural in some way?

KMC: It's combined, they are interwoven.

ST: Is that something that is still informing your on-going work?

KMC: That will probably be with me for the rest of my life. My association with architects has been fraught insofar as they seem to enjoy the attention, they're happy that poets discover them, but then they prove to be too busy to really collaborate in a meaningful way. Architects aren't proving as rewarding as their work! The same can be said of poets…

ST: Indeed! Would you like to collaborate with an architect on a building and/or text or some kind of hybrid?

KMC: Yes. I would like to be able to think about structure in the way that an architect can think about a construct. I suppose I can do that with poetry to a certain extent. I think all of us as writers are capable of that.

ST: For Allen Fisher, deconstruction in architecture is one of his key reference points.

KMC: Yes, I would like to see how much further it could go. I think inherently I'm a curious person. I'm interested in lots of different things and I read in different areas. I'm interested in what happens or what might happen when you put certain things together that aren't usually thought of as necessarily compatible. Sometimes they're not compatible, sometimes it doesn't work. But when it does, it produces a new way of looking at things, hopefully.

[*End of London interview*]

Talking Poetics

ST: I found John Hall's essay on your work particularly useful in the distinction he makes between poetry driven by ontology and poetry driven by knowledge.[13] It links to my written question to you[14] about the status and function of poetry in relation to other discourses—does it have a special status, is it a distinct form of thought?

KMC: Well, surely each form is distinct in its own right, each form of thought, whether it be mathematical, philosophical, poetical. These are different vocabularies. But I think what you're asking me, really, is poetry for me a privileged form of thought? And, yes, it is. We live within language, language is our primary environment and even when we're not communicating, there is still this intense awareness, at least on my part, of what language is doing. That's why I was so struck today in the stacks at the Poetry Collection[15] when I saw "W ends", remember that sign "W ends"? [**ST**: Yes!] For me that was a wonderful moment because if "w ends", it also begins and it has a middle too, and maybe it's more open-ended than that!

So does this characterize poetic thinking? I would say perhaps it does, because surely poetry is the way one experiences and appreciates language in a specific form. So yes, poetry for me is a privileged form of thought, but I'm also intent on finding out what happens to poetry and different discourses when they are brought into the same field. Which is why I have gone to various shorthand manuals, typewriter manuals and tried to both integrate and align (very self-consciously) these different forms of thought. And what does that do to our notion of what poetic thought is, can it accommodate other discourses? What happens when you bring disciplines together? This is often referred to as "inter-disciplinary". Marcos Novak came up with the term "trans-disciplinary" which is his preference. One always runs the risk of turning "inter"/"trans" into something unsatisfactory for *both* (or multiple) disciplines. Therein the danger lies. Does one rely too

---

[13] "There is a writing driven by and towards an ontology, a discourse on *being* [...] this kind of writing wants to be at once singular and universal. [...] And then—and here is a first distinction—there is a writing that knowingly operates in nets and modes of knowledge. It might well do so in a spirit of disputation [...] to disturb vectors of knowledge. [...] There is an extreme form of this position in writing, and one with which I'd connect Karen Mac Cormack: any act of writing, even the purportedly ontological, intervenes in knowledge". Hall, 'Karen Mac Cormack's *Implexures*', pp. 231–32.

[14] I had sent a number of written questions to Mac Cormack in advance of this part of the interview.

[15] The Poetry Collection at The State University of New York, Buffalo. Mac Cormack and I visited on Wednesday 7 April 2009.

much on what one already knows or does one misapply things, thinking the "result" wonderful when somebody else who knows another discipline better would disagree? I suppose whenever an attempt is made with inter-disciplinary or trans-disciplinary practice, there is that danger.

ST: But clearly one that for you is worth entertaining at least to a degree?

KMC: I have found it to be incredibly productive. I don't know if everybody would agree with that. Some people look at my work—yes, they look at it, they don't read it—and decree that it doesn't make sense. Well, on the contrary it makes sense, in the plural, of senses. It's not singular, at least I don't consider it working in the singular of meaning, rather "meanings".

ST: I think once you can accept the formal decisions that are being made, there are passages which are very clear. If we're talking about *Implexures*...

KMC: I'd apply that to my work in its entirety. Actually I'd like to ask you a question since you bravely decided to include an excerpt from *Implexures* on one of the courses you teach—what did your students make of it?

ST: We looked at the very first section and the section where you refer to the opening of *A Thousand Plateaus*, which we were also engaging with. They didn't quite know what to say initially, but then they started to find little ways in for themselves. They started to notice the difference in the textures, for example the extract from the St Lucia travelogue. It stands out, so they noticed that here's something different being inserted. Once they'd gotten over the initial difficulty as they perceived it, they were quite accepting of it, that here's a text that's assimilating different elements. One student in particular I think has grasped in a basic but solid way the possibilities of that for his own writing—how energy is released when one brings those things into relation.

I wonder whether poetry is special because it can absorb multiple discourses and forge a relation to them, whereas a mathematical equation with poetry in it is unlikely to work as mathematics.

KMC: Well, perhaps we don't understand the language of maths sufficiently. Apparently there are mathematical "jokes" but the lay person sees only a string of numbers and letters and can't ask for it to be explained because that would probably require a two-hour response.

ST: And then there are levels of understanding that one simply can't just step-up to in actual fact, that it would be more like two years than two hours, because of the time it takes to absorb a style of thought. It's like the way in which an artist who makes a mark on a canvas can imbue just a simple pencil stroke with extraordinarily delicate overtones and there's only one way to reach that level of skill which is just to keep doing it for years and years.

KMC: In that case then, poetry's relationship to language is special because it does for language what dance does for movement. Forms of thought are discussed in/through language. Dance *and* poetry? I haven't seen enough of that. I know that Sally Silvers and Bruce Andrews have collaborated, but I personally haven't seen any of those performances. Steve [Mc Caffery] has worked with dancers. I suppose the challenge is how to make the poetic line integrate with the rhythm of a dance movement in a mutually evocative space. I don't know of many people working with this.

ST: When I'm looking at other disciplines and their complexity I'm often creatively jealous of them. But I see it as a challenge to think, well, what's distinct about the mode of thought that I'm engaging in and what are the highest reaches of its discipline? What is its integrity as a mode of thinking?

KMC: Well, it's not only a mode of thinking, it's a mode of expression, because it's a combination not only of intellectual thinking, but also everything else that poetry does.

ST: Yes. I'm using "thinking" as a shorthand really, but yes, it's emotion, it's the non-verbal, and it's as much about our relationship to language as anything else. But I'm interested in trying to grasp the actual movement of thought itself. I wonder whether it can be separated from all of these ways in which humans undertake to describe or represent their relationship to the world.

KMC: It's a big question. I would propose that what poetry does for expression—and I'm not going to use shorthand—is that perhaps poetry is the creative *rocade* to language that allows different forms of expression to arise within language. Now, the *rocade* is the Knight's move in chess,[16] as

---

[16] The move is defined as: "first one step in a horizontal or vertical direction, and then one step diagonally in an outward direction. The knight *jumps*: it is allowed that the first square that the knight passes over is occupied by an arbitrary piece". See www.chessvariants.org/d.chess/chess.html, accessed 22 December 2008.

well as being a bypass; it's not a linear move, it's what happens when you turn in another (specific) direction. Perhaps that's what poetry can be to language ... and the poetic forms—the poems that result—inform poetics. And that makes poetry special. But again we live with so many different forms of poetry. When I think of visual or concrete poetry, it's that flash of recognition or that sudden surprise that is so wonderful about visual work. But how poetry functions within spoken word or any oral tradition is very different. The Inuit throat singers don't consider themselves poets, but their performances are appreciated around the world at poetry and music festivals. For them it's a form of relaxation in-between tasks. So perhaps we're going off in too many directions, I suppose we'll find out when this is transcribed!

ST: It's okay, along the way we're actually defining a broader area of thinking about these problems.

KMC: When you think about poetry that doesn't work with words, as in visual or concrete, we still refer to it as poetry. Why? Because it's a strategy, it does something that we consider poetic, but it does it differently because it's a different medium if you will.

ST: But whatever that relationship to space and meaning that the visual poem can generate, you could talk about it in mathematical terms if you were analyzing its spatial geometry, for example, or you could talk about in architectural terms in terms of constructed space, or you could talk about in terms of perceptual phenomena and how one receives information and makes it cohere in some way.

KMC: Well, perhaps it would be helpful to remind ourselves that a distinction is made between poets who create concrete and visual work and visual artists who include language in their visual art work. So if you look at say, Jenny Holzer's work, do you respond by saying "how poetic!"? I don't. Because I think that it comes out of a visual arts practice.

ST: It always feels distinct to me when that's going on.

KMC: But what happens when one looks at Cy Twombly's work, for example?

ST: Yes, that's poetic! Without the words. Or actually sometimes with words as well!

KMC: So again, we can make distinctions, but so often there is an exception, and the *rocade* has occurred again. If this process of the *rocade* continues, can one follow the trajectory of sorts or does one end up back in the same spot? I'm really not sure. I'm thinking out loud at this stage. But it seems to me a productive approach to wonder what happens next, or to push it that much further, to create a different move. Because, again, as soon as something becomes habitual… Surely part of poetry, poetics and being a poet is developing an ability, not of surprise itself, but ongoingly the ability *to* surprise and challenge oneself. I made a distinction between "project-to-project" artists and "railroad" artists. The railroad artist discovers what s/he is good at and continues with variations for the rest of his or her creative life. The "project-to-project" artist goes about a series of work, may not produce another series for a while, but when she or he does, it's engaging with different concerns, possibly in different media. That is what I appreciate most of the time.

ST: It's a really good analogy. It reminds me of something the Polish writer Witold Gombrowicz said of the task of writing that, to summarise crudely, one ought to be prepared to allow whatever issues one has to be expressed without judgement, so that even if it's not particularly effective, one can still value it as part of the ongoing process.[17] For me that would link to the project-based way of approaching things. Is it a temperamental thing? Would you admire railroaders?

KMC: Oh, certainly.

ST: So you wouldn't ultimately privilege one over the other?

KMC: I think that the railroad artists, if they are to produce successful successive variations, then they're still challenging themselves, they're still exploring further, they're developing their craft. It's just that they're not challenging themselves to do anything else. They are on a mission to perfect their art form. Whereas personally I am more interested in seeing what happens when one isn't as comfortable with a particular form. If you are a writer of sonnets and you write beautiful sonnets and you continue to write even lovelier sonnets, that's fantastic but what would happen if you wrote a villanelle instead, for example?

---

[17] Gombrowicz refers to this as a "process of becoming". See Witold Gombrowicz, *Ferdydurke* (1938) (New Haven, CT and London: Yale University Press, 2000), p. 82.

ST: Or if you wrote a narrative poem or a visual poem?

KMC: Many years ago I knew a visual artist [Michael Collins] who challenged himself by doing a series of works on paper using his left hand, and he was right-handed. Not his best work, but it was intriguing.

ST: That comes back to that Gombrowicz thing—that sometimes you just need to keep things moving. He had a real beef about poets in general, responding specifically to the cultural conditions of his time. He was reacting to people just in love with the idea of being a poet.[18]

KMC: Ah, the Romantic notion of what a poet is and how they exist!

ST: Yes, which he lacerated very convincingly. For him the writer needed to be constantly capable of adapting to different conditions. It's almost like allowing oneself to be stupid if that's what the situation honestly demands or that's just what occurs. That you say well, that's good, I've done something stupid so it's allowed myself to release that part of me that *is* stupid and now I can take the next step.[19]

KMC: Oh, I wish it were that simple! [laughter] I think our stupidity returns more often than we would like it to!

ST: You're right! But I find that quite liberating because it says you don't have to keep to the railroad.

KMC: But if you choose to make that public, then that isn't so liberating. There is a lot of self-indulgent work by artists out there already. I'm using the term artist rather than poet because I think it applies across disciplines.

ST: That's absolutely true. But maybe the difference is really subtle. It might be a railroad but look like a series of projects or a series of projects might look like a railroad. It might just be in how the person is addressing whatever is actually being produced at the time that would determine how much they are challenging themselves.

---

[18] See 'Against Poets' in Witold Gombrowicz, *Diary Volume One: 1953–1956* (London and New York: Quartet Books, 1988), pp. 215–222.
[19] I am alluding here to a passage in Gombrowicz's *Ferdydurke*: "'Great! I've written something stupid, but I haven't signed a contract with anyone to produce solely wise and perfect works. I gave vent to my stupidity and I'm glad of it, because the animosity and harshness of others that I've aroused against me will now form and shape me, it will create me as if anew, and here I am—reborn'", p. 82.

KMC: Yes, because people who work non-stop with constraint generate things that look different or read differently, but if you only work within constraint then...

ST: It becomes a railroad.

[Break]

ST: To return to this distinction John Hall makes between writing driven by ontology and writing driven by knowledge, do you see that as a useful distinction for the way you think about your work? Hall identifies your practice with the latter.

KMC: Can one be without the other? I mean humankind can, in terms of history, but an individual? It comes with the territory.

ST: I'm recalling now that he sees *Implexures* as "at once ontological, epistemological and narratorial",[20] but I suppose I identify your work more with epistemology.

KMC: Well, I would say that it's perhaps necessary as a way of thinking about the project *Implexures*, rather than as an approach by a writer to a project, especially to a project of this nature. I did not deliberately set up a distinction between ontology and knowledge and I didn't write through each, thinking to juxtapose them or bring them together to collide and do whatever they might do. But in hindsight, I can understand why he wrote what he did, and I think that perhaps that is more useful to potential readers or those readers who have been puzzled by the work.

ST: Actually it would be tremendously useful for teaching with.

KMC: From a critical point of view it seems extremely apt and insightful. From the creative perspective, it's interesting to see it laid out that way, and I'm grateful to him for that essay, tremendously grateful to him, but for me as an experience it wasn't like that.

ST: I can accept that completely because my understanding of your work is that you're not going into it with that approach.

---

[20] Hall, 'Karen Mac Cormack's *Implexures*', p. 233.

KMC: How does one situate the outline of a construction, or the phases of development in any project, poetic or otherwise? I look back on the writing of *Implexures*, I suppose more than anything else, with some amazement. For one thing, it occupied so much more of my life than any other project. I will say that after I ceased working on it I felt the need to turn to shorter forms.

ST: Yes, there're some in *Veer Off*.[21]

KMC: They're concise, just a few lines some of them ... but I don't know if they reflect a "resting" moment or signal a different attention to temporality, duration, and space. I don't see why I wouldn't write a longer work again, whether a poem or something else. I do not intend to continue *Implexures*. For me, despite the fact that it could be an open-ended project, I don't see my relation to it as open-ended. You ask in one of your questions, "what didn't go into *Implexures*?" and "why does creativity challenge us to make connections?" I responded initially by writing: [reads] "what didn't go into *Implexures* could quite possibly result in other volumes if I intended to continue the project. Much of the material in some way wasn't as provocative or evocative, or was too painful either for me personally, or for others still living". It did reach a point where I had to consider how prepared I was to include, for example, juvenilia, which for me to read might still be interesting, given that I can recognise a development towards my ways of writing now. As I said earlier, there's a lot out there that is self-indulgent. I'm thinking of the works that are published simply because someone is or was famous. If the name is taken away then the question becomes "why is this in print?" Or "why has this recording become available?"

ST: That comes back to that Gombrowicz thing for me. I think one of the things I was trying to test in *Momentum* as a book was how much I could push my voice into different voices—separate voices, as the middle section's called—and just trust that the integrity of the whole process would somehow sustain that errant impulse to write the poem that doesn't or couldn't, but still does, sit alongside the other ones, even though it's taking an entirely different approach to its material.

---

[21] 'About Slant', 'arco iris', 'arcobaleno' and 'for H.B.' appeared in *Veer Off / Veer* 15 (October 2008), 117–120. Republished in Karen Mac Cormack, *Tale Light: New and Selected Poems 1984–2009* (Toronto and Sheffield: Book Thug and West House Books, 2010), pp. 181-84.

KMC: Why should we limit ourselves to a single voice? We don't exist in a single sense but in multiple senses. This notion of a writer finding his or her "own" voice is completely alien to me. If you can't embrace the diversity and multiplicity of possibilities that exist in terms of voices, then surely your experience as a writer is diminished as a result of that limitation. This returns us (via a *rocade?*) to the difference between a railroad artist and a project-to-project artist. I suppose that there are some who fall midway between, or that there are gradations even within that: those who start off being more inclined to the one and then become the other, and vice-versa.

ST: It's a fascinating dynamic because, to me, it encompasses something about how style exists word to word: that there are those who will emphasize continuities in a piece and those who will emphasize discontinuities. It's almost a macro-version of that. John had a nice phrase about *Implexures*— that it was not only polybiographical, but it was also polymodal.[22]

KMC: Yes. Perhaps that's why I so appreciate Raymond Queneau's *Exercises in Style*.[23] When I read that, many years ago, I especially appreciated the fact that this writer is really exploring a range of possibilities. And even if he were never to do so again in any other work, somehow that process, that engagement, must have informed all his subsequent writing.

ST: So you've investigated the possibilities in a really full way. I'm very interested in that. I guess it's not so obvious on a formal level, but for me it's much more about treating each poem as a completely new opportunity.

KMC: That's a lovely way to put it. If you embrace that completely new opportunity that each poem provides, and how far you take it is up to you, obviously.

ST: And not thinking about what the last poem was. Just really being in the present and trying to be worthy or equal to whatever happens, to whatever material's on the table. What was so intriguing about being with the Joyce notebooks yesterday in the Poetry Collection[24] was recognizing the way I use notebooks for collecting materials that then go into the poem

---

[22] Hall, 'Karen Mac Cormack's *Implexures*', p. 241.
[23] Queneau's famous book comprises ninety-nine retellings of the same very short story featuring a character who complains to a fellow passenger on a bus and then is seen by the narrator two hours later being told he needs a new button on his coat. It was first published in 1947.
[24] Wednesday 7 April 2009.

Karen Mac Cormack

and the process of selection. I liked the fact that Joyce was putting a line through something when it had been taken up.

KMC: And different colours in terms of crayons and subsequent placement of material in *Finnegans Wake*—very important aspect!

ST: Yes, and there are sixty-five of these that are presumably all in play at different times. For me, I keep one notebook which is always ongoing and if I'm writing a poem a week, which I more or less manage to do, then it's whatever material is available that hasn't been used basically, plus whatever book's in hand that I'm reading precisely for material, and then it all gets managed into a piece there and then. But what seemed to be Joyce's way was that it's just on a different scale, that he's accumulating.

KMC: Yes, there were multiple notebooks: there were the tiny ones which would fit in his pocket which he might have taken with him to the café. Then there were the larger ones, and perhaps they were scattered all over the place. I don't know, I'm not a Joyce scholar, but my experience of those notebooks over the years—and I don't go to them non-stop but certainly I return to them again and again in different contexts—is one of the possibility of working in more than one notebook at a time. I decided on a new notebook when I began my research on the Kathleen Cannell archive at Harvard University, and I tend to keep that separate because I'm going to return to that material, but it could be that other things find their way into that. My present notebook I began at both ends accidentally. So I gave it a title of "meet in the middle" just as a reminder to myself that I was writing in both directions towards the middle of the notebook. So these are slightly different strategies. I do not like keying in a poem on a computer from scratch, I don't sit in front of the screen and compose. I tend to work on paper.

ST: That's my preference as well. How long does it remain in that state though before you start to type it up?

KMC: Varies. Sometimes I'll start keying something in, and I may want to add to it and I may do so on screen. But I don't think I've ever commenced writing anything by opening a file on a computer. To return to your question about *Implexures,* John Hall said something very interesting in conversation when we visited him in June 2008. Steve asked if I would work towards another volume of *Implexures,* and I answered in the negative. John Hall's assertion was that the method of *Implexures* would probably be with me forever—or words to that effect. How I act upon that, where I might extend or shift it, or allow the *rocade* to take it in a different direction, remains to be seen.

ST: Yes, he makes a distinction between your use of the fold and a Deleuzian use of it, but what he's more comfortable with is closer to a geological sense or even a culinary sense of folding.[25] But how much does the Deleuzian concept inform your work? We talked about the fold and the fan before.

KMC: Yes, there are so many different kinds of fold, Deleuzian and otherwise.

ST: There's that passage that illustrates a version of it: on the semiotics of the fan.[26]

KMC: Ah, the language of the fan.

ST: It's a passage I would use to illustrate this practice were I writing about it critically, because the fan is both a theme here as well as a model for some of the processes of thinking about time.[27] I think it's because one can see the grain of the continuity of the text about fan language and that creates a sort of local ground against which one can see other ingredients standing out, like a line of quartz in a block of granite, folded in a particular way.

KMC: If this particular section were to be presented as a visual poem or passage, it would indeed indicate the experience of what happens when you drop a fan, when you then open it up, and when you allow it to close very carefully. Now we're referring to the *folding* fan. There's a French eighteenth century fan upstairs, and a Chinese nineteenth century one, and then there's the flat Japanese fan that doesn't fold. I became obsessed with different kinds of fans, and even what the shape of a fan does to the air-currents when one is actually fanning oneself, when I was writing *Implexures*.

But to get to your question regarding how influential Deleuze and Guattari might have been, I did not sit down and read *Mille Plateaux* from cover to cover in order to arrive at an appreciation of their work as cited in *Implexures* or elsewhere. I read in many different areas and I become

---

[25] Hall, 'Karen Mac Cormack's *Implexures*', p. 242.
[26] Mac Cormack, *Implexures*, p. 92.
[27] Mac Cormack, *Implexures*, p. 17.

excited about many different things and I want to bring that excitement to my readers. Sometimes readers consider my approach too scattered, others go with the text to discover where it takes them. It was Steve who actually commented about the amount of information in *Implexures*. That hadn't occurred to me and nobody else has commented on that that I can recall in terms of reviews or essays. Most people focus on what is going on within the work.

ST: Yes, and it's information that one can actually use, in a sense. It's not like it's so fragmented that it doesn't have any integrity left.

KMC: But it's information that is presented in a new context, or alongside other contexts. That is why I'm still so interested in the notion of the trans- and the inter-disciplinary or the abutment of discourses that aren't necessarily compatible, and what you do in that moment when you realize that something either works or it doesn't. It's the way in which Deleuze and Guattari can inform forms of thought other than their own field of the philosophical. Similarly, Cache's notion of the fold in architecture is different from the range of notions of folding that appear in *Implexures*. 'Machicolated Conversations' is an exploration of what happens when different discourses share a given space. In that sense it's not a folding, it's an encounter.

ST: So none of this has been published yet?

KMC: The first of the series appeared in *New American Writing* last year, but no, I haven't sent much of it out into the world as yet.

ST: It may be just a way into finding out more about architecture which will lead into the 'Innovation's Inventory' essay, but I would like to know about what drew you to Cache's work.

KMC: Steve and I both read about Cache in relation to Deleuze. I wanted to find out what this architect did with the fold and I discovered that his *vector–inflection–frame*[28] approach offered me different possibilities. If multiple *vector–inflection–frame* moments were folded together or introduced at different intervals, what would that look like in terms of poetry? So that was my primary interest in his work. I continue to read

---

[28] See Bernard Cache, *Earth Moves*, translated by Anne Boyman (Cambridge, MA: The MIT Press, 1995), p. 1.

books on architecture, but none of them as interesting as that particular work (at least thus far).

ST: I can grasp vector as a line of movement, but I don't understand what inflection might be.

KMC: Well, if one thinks of working on a poem, the vector would be one's consideration of how one is going to arrive at what goes into a line, so it's more of a reference to the composition, at least in my thinking. The inflection would be what actually ends up in one's word choice, or how one is determining one's word choice. Then the frame would be how each line of a poem appears, in print form. And one would revisit this process when one edits a poem or any other work. It doesn't have so much to do with how poetry appears on the page: you wouldn't isolate vector, inflection and frame. It's the creative process of the poet that's engaged.

ST: That's really clear. Does that have some connection with the relationship between the actual and the virtual?

KMC: It has a sense, for me, that the drafts of a poem would represent a moving from the virtual to the actual. But that's really specific to my practice. I haven't read Cache in some time, although I have a file full of copious notes on *Earth Moves*. But I'm tremendously interested in all forms of eco-architecture. Did you find any of the work of Shigeru Ban, the Japanese architect?

ST: Yes I did. Beautiful buildings!

KMC: He created an ingenious solution for temporary housing after the Kobe earthquake. He works with recycled cardboard and creates these structures out of prefabricated components.

ST: That reminds me of Buckminster Fuller, whom you mention briefly in a footnote in the 'Innovation's Inventory' essay. The Dymaxion work. He was very interested in prefabrication: semi-permanent structures that could be put up in a few hours and even picked up and moved somewhere else.

KMC: Perhaps this is why I am so drawn to tents as a form of architecture, and the nomadic lifestyle. Frei Otto, for example, is a German architect who worked with tents and pavilion structures. I first became aware of his work in the 1970s. The idea that nomads in certain parts of the world can put up a structure overnight and take it away with them the next day is, to me, quite magical. Even the Inuit do this with their ice-houses. They will build the igloo, as it can be maintained in winter; not that there are many igloos being built anymore, unfortunately. But I am preoccupied by that whole relationship between the necessary and the fact that it can just disappear the next minute. It dispenses in a strange way with the notion of the fragment, because even the ice can melt away, the sands can cover anything that might have been left. Obviously climate provides a specific condition! But I suppose for me that is a manifestation of the creative act: it can appear and just as quickly disappear.

ST: There was a lovely phrase in Cache to do with the frame of probability, that the page or the stage or the frame creates the probability of writing or dance or movement.[29] It's as if one is drawn to a blank space where nothing is evident because it contains the possibility that something will arrive and then move on. But when you present a book you're obliged to have all of that together: maybe that's where you're looking for other solutions? However, I can't just go to a room and give one poem for that time, and then it disappears, although it would be quite interesting to do that!

KMC: Well, in a sense we have that capability now. We enjoy that capability, or perhaps it's something other than a capability. Some people would see it as a detriment, but one can now read books on a computer. In that sense it increases the ephemerality, because one is no longer relying on the weight of the printed page, literally. But then what to do with books that won't necessarily be consulted again? What happens to them? And what if one lets them go only to suddenly realise they're necessary after all?

We can now access technology that would allow us to store that work, but to experience it in an utterly different way, because to read a work, any work, on a computer screen, is, at least for this writer and reader, different from holding the book in the hand. It is closer to the scroll, which is how most writing began, but it opens up different possibilities. When I see what's being done with flash and visual poetry—obviously Brian Kim-Stefans is the name that first comes to mind—that's tremendously exciting. But we are now at a period in the history of humankind where we really do need to consider whether we should be producing as many print editions as we do. But that really is off in another direction from what we've been discussing.

---

[29] Cache, *Earth Moves*, p. 23, 25.

ST: Perhaps that's the cue to focus on exactly what you are saying about your relationship with architecture in 'Innovation's Inventory'. There was quite a striking articulation of this poetry of "<<is>>", with <<is>> as a "constantly shifting 'particular'".[30] I was trying to understand the significance of the marks around "is".

KMC: That is directly related to Gins and Arakawa and how <<is>> appears in one of their works, which I refer to in 'Innovation's Inventory'.[31] For me, it's about the present tense, and how one defines the present tense. If one is going to think about what it means to be in the world, then the present tense moves obviously from one spacetime moment to the next, although that's too linear a way of putting it! Our experience doesn't move in a linear way. In that sense I really do agree with both Bergson and Bachelard, that we experience spacetime in durations of intensity: those hours when one experiences the feeling of boredom, and each second seems an eternity, or when one is involved in intense intellectual or creative or emotional or physical activity and time evaporates so quickly. And then what happens if experience exceeds time? You were asking about this in your written questions.

ST: Yes, about expansion and contraction. In *Implexures* you write: "which intensity reinforced by memory, when the moment exceeds time, simultaneously expands and contracts space?"[32]

KMC: The dynamics of contraction and expansion and emotion.

ST: I was linking that expansion and contraction to the body in terms of breath.

KMC: Well, for me, it's not only the body and breath, although certainly the body and breath are involved. It's the immensity of what occurs when expansion is such a dominant force that one can't imagine contraction, yet, of course, contraction eventually comes. And what that means in

---

[30] Karen Mac Cormack, 'Innovation's Inventory' (revised version of an essay first published in *Architectures of Poetry* edited by Maria Eugenia Diaz and Craig Douglas Dworkin, Amsterdam and New York: Rodopi, 2004), p. 8.
[31] Ibid., p. 8. The Arakawa and Madeline Gins text referred to is 'Pour ne pas mourir / To Not To Die', trans. by François Rosso, (Paris: Éditions de la Différence, 1987).
[32] Mac Cormack, *Implexures*, p. 68. See also p. 119: "an event whose moment, though differing with each individual, in a sense exceeds the temporal even as it localizes its force upon each life".

emotional and creative and intellectual terms and how one can evoke this for a reader—in our case because we're poets—and *can* one? That's one of the concerns that informs *Implexures* in particular but also my work in general. There was another part to your question, about the family and the expanded model of identity, the poetics of relationships.

ST: I hadn't actually realized that I was asking about expansion in both.

KMC: Yes, you did. So this expansion and contraction, I don't think of it as a poetics of relationships myself, and as I wrote in my initial response, it's a bit like that aspect that John Hall delineates as ontology versus knowledge—it wasn't something that was self-conscious as part of the creative or intellectual processes that were at work. But it was something that one can perhaps formulate or articulate after the fact, when one looks at that work.

ST: Barrett Watten's definition of method is that which is understood after the writing has taken place—technique is what drives the process, and method is what begins with the finished work.

KMC: Well, I think in my case it would be that exploration is what drives the process, not simply technique. Technique is something that appears or becomes apparent during the course of exploring the process. Whatever reasons one articulates in terms of why a poet works on a particular project with these particular concerns is—for this writer—not always something that is entirely "known" in advance, as we've already discussed earlier in this interview. In *Implexures* poetic forces are brought to bear on prose.

I can say these things now after the fact. If you had asked me various questions while I was working on that project, I don't know if I would have been able to answer you. Perhaps that's something lacking in me, not recognizing precisely what it is that I'm doing, or perhaps it's just the way I function as a writer, that I need to keep certain things open because I want other things to be able to come into the project and the process. If there is something else that can inform it, then I welcome that. Whereas I think that certain other writers or artists have clearly determined ideas as to what they are going to do, how they are going to go about it, and the techniques that they need to employ. I think that just says something about one person's creativity coming into being in a way different from others'.

ST: For myself, if I solve the problems I'm trying to explore in creative work by other means it risks undoing the creative process. Having said that, if I'm in the middle of something, I'm not really in a position to theorize it because it's still underway. Although I might be trying to grasp all manner of things in order to do it, I can't really talk about it until it's finished.

KMC: Or if you do, and it actually goes into a print interview, i.e. a published interview, you might look back on it and say by the time I decided to stop working on that project I felt differently and I would have answered these questions very differently. Because I don't think we ever "stop". I don't think a project is ever finished. One decides to cease working on something. One arrives at a moment when one says, "I can let this go out into the world and see what happens". Marianne Moore of course is a famous example of a poet who would rework her poems and publish them in their revised forms years later. Which to me is interesting—it allows your readership to follow your own process in an interesting way.

ST: I'm fascinated by that. When I was working on Adrian Clarke's writing I was comparing successive appearances of his poems. And Adrian now is doing things like revising books which are ten or fifteen years old and cropping them down to a tenth of their original length. To return to the 'Innovation's Inventory' essay, you ask two questions of yourself in parentheses: "does this make language itself an architectural encounter too?" and "so poetry represents a meaningful particular architecting of and through language by perplexing it?"[33]

KMC: I continue to ask myself those questions. It shifts. It has shifted since I originally wrote that, and the more I experience architectural discourse and occasionally when meeting various architects, other factors are introduced. It was Steve's notion that language is our primary environment. We live within language, we express ourselves through language. We also express ourselves through music, dance and the visual arts, to name but a few, though we discuss all these experiences, or these different practices, in language or through language: so dance is reviewed by putting words to paper, or on a computer screen. We were talking about what poetry "is" earlier, so why can't it be—I know "architecting" is a horrible verb—but could it be a way of "architecting"!?

---

[33] Mac Cormack, 'Innovation's Inventory', p. 8, 9.

Karen Mac Cormack

ST: This makes me wonder about the etymology of the word "architecture".

KMC: It would be the making of buildings, I suppose.[34] But it's always a creation. So is poetry a particular way of creating with language?

ST: You put it in your conclusion that: "I'm now considering 'poetry' as almost a particular assemblage of perceptual angles, degrees, and vectors even, in what is the process of creative ideas being constructed through and in and in relation to language".[35]

KMC: Which made perfect sense to me at the time. I seek out architectural discourse and ideas and developments, but my closeness or distance to that statement varies.

ST: I still find it quite a striking declaration.

KMC: It takes poetry off a two-dimensional surface, let's put it that way, and it challenges the notion that poetry is something that appears primarily on the page. But of course, as we discussed earlier, with oral traditions, it's either handed down from one generation to the next or it's on tape, recorded.

ST: But then it seems to me that there's another space entirely that you're evoking here which I imagine as, rather than walking through architectural space, that one walks through linguistic space and encounters it in an almost physical way.

KMC: Well, linguistic *forms*, actually, to be more specific, rather than linguistic space. There's also that possibility, as we were discussing earlier, of what happens when one form of thought or process encounters another. What if you have two linguistic forms juxtaposed on the same "page"?

ST: Ah, this is the "conversations", isn't it? Dialogue. And "machicolated" is this particular structure. So what is it about that that you're interested in as an architectural idea, is it because it's a form of boundary?

KMC: Well, that informs the process. I'm more interested in the fact that because there are apertures there is the possibility for entrances as well as exits. As I said, I don't know how many of these poems will result from this

---

[34] According to the *Online Etymological Dictionary*, Greek *arkhitekton* "master builder", from *arkhi-* 'chief' (see *archon*) + *tekton* "builder, carpenter" (see *texture*). See http://www.etymonline.com, consulted 22 November, 2010.
[35] Mac Cormack, 'Innovation's Inventory', p. 10.

particular investigation, but it's my present preoccupation!

ST: When you were talking about this notion of poetry as an architecting of language—language as an architectural encounter—that connected for me with Michel de Certeau's work on walking in the city, which he frames in terms of synecdoche and asyndeton.[36] I've used this to write about *le parkour* in relation to Ulli Freer's work[37] which might also connect to the way Arakawa and Gins talk about the body in action.[38] I wonder if architecture is still a useful word at that point, if we're talking about the body in action?

KMC: When one considers the thinking about how bodies in action do and don't relate to architecture it does raise the question of what kind of architecture we are talking about—the architecture of language or physical architecture? But there's a Michel de Certeau quotation I remember including as an epigraph to one of my books (*Marine Snow*): "There will thus be facts that are no longer truths". That to me was absolutely wonderful because of course the definition of something and/or our understanding of how something "works" can change over time because what was thought of as being accurate initially, might be proven to be wrong. It's this wonderful moment when there's a transition in terms of meaning and understanding... this occurs more often than we like to think it does. The shifting of how meaning emerges and disappears is to me an endless source of fascination. Perhaps I should just leave it at that!

ST: It's not a bad note to end on! It just reminded me of something John Hall said about meaning as a desire for sense in his essay: "let me call 'meaning', for a moment, and in this context, nothing other than an insatiable desire for sense".[39]

---

[36] Michel de Certeau, *The Practice of Everyday Life*, translated by Steven F. Rendall (Berkeley, CA: University of California Press, 1984), p. 101.
[37] See Scott Thurston, 'Ulli Freer: Space is the Place', *Poetry Salzburg Review* 9 (Spring 2006), pp. 180–187.
[38] "If the basic unit of concern is the body, not an abstract body considered apart from impulses and movement, but the body in action, then will not the concepts most central to the living of a life be those formed—no matter how fleetingly—through architectural encounters?" Arakawa and Madeline Gins in Charles W. Haxthausen, *Reversible Destiny* (New York: Guggenheim Museum Publications, 1997), p. 29, cited in Mac Cormack, 'Innovation's Inventory', p. 8.
[39] Hall, 'Mac Cormack's *Implexures*', p. 243.

Jennifer Moxley

This interview was conducted at Jennifer Moxley's house in Orono, Maine, from 10 to 12 April 2009.

Scott Thurston: I've been fascinated for years by the tension between a pair of terms I got from Barrett Watten's *Total Syntax*, where he was trying to address the problem of what can happen to procedural writing when the procedure takes over. He called that *technique*—the part of the writing that is to do with how you're doing it—which he contrasted with *method*, which is more about why you do it, and how the work is implicated in the larger socio-cultural world.[1] Watten felt that too many of his contemporaries were fetishizing technique at the expense of method, and finding it hard to move forward. When I discovered his distinction in the late 90s I thought it described my own situation as a writer quite well and thus it became very useful for my development. I wonder if you could say something about your own approach to composition in the context of that?

Jennifer Moxley: I agree with Barrett's argument a hundred percent because—and this is something Nicole Brossard talks about as well—there's got to be a motive. To have a technique just to have one, like a poem machine, risks being an under-motivated formal gesture. You can create a structure and fill it, but why? Why does the work need to be in the world? There has to be a kind of existential urgency for me in both the poems I write and the poems I read. I do not want to sense that the poet has too much time on their hands and is just filling structures.

Which is not to say that poems that work with predetermined structures or techniques are always going to be unmotivated. No, because someone like Jackson Mac Low is fascinating at every point. He can take a system and come up with something fascinating, whereas I imagine another poet could use the same system and it wouldn't be interesting at all. So that's the little mystery that technique doesn't explain. But I feel that you must feel urgently connected to your formal choices, and not just say well that's what everyone's doing so I'm going to do that.

ST: I think it often gets settled by temperament. You can think these decisions through as much as you like, but some things just work better for you than others and there's not necessarily a reason why. Or at least that's

---

[1] See Barrett Watten, *Total Syntax* (Carbondale and Edwardsville: Southern Illinois University Press, 1985), p. 32. See also pp. 7–8, p. 44 and p. 86.

my experience.

JM: Yes, exactly. A scholar friend once told me a story about a poet who admitted to erasing the last line of every poem in order to avoid having closure. Perhaps this poet came up with better poems in each case, but to make a unilateral decision, "I refuse to have closure" violates the process. What if those poems were meant to have closure? Wouldn't it be wrong to erase that event?

ST: The rejection of closure no less!

JM: Yes. I think it's more interesting if your poems are doing something you don't consciously intend, to leave it in and think about why it's happening. If your poem does something that doesn't match up with your ideology, you shouldn't go back and pretend it didn't happen and change it. I value the fact that my work might evolve in a way that does not agree with my stated ideology or beliefs. It might tell me things that are unpleasant or unpopular, but to pretend that those things are not there is to deny something important.

ST: I think there's that part of writing that can sometimes, if you're really following the logic of the work, lead you to places that you wouldn't otherwise sanction under other conditions. Recent developments in my writing have been about allowing myself to leave those things in and not to deny them or remove them because they don't fit with the kind of poet I think I am or should be or whom others want me to be.

JM: It's like love. Well, maybe not love so much but *desire*. Sometimes I desire in a way that is not correct, and that I know is not correct, but which I nevertheless find interesting—why am I desiring in this way? I like to note such moments and learn from them. That's why I mentioned Nicole Brossard, because she's a poet who has really thought a lot about desire, but she has a much more politicized version of desire: she's been very active about female desire as an intervention into patriarchy. But I'm not talking in that sense, I'm just saying that as much as you are socially conditioned or repressed, there are always little cracks, there are always little things that come out, and that it is important to notice those. Likewise, in my creative work, I include things that I should by all rights edit out, but I don't.

ST: I appreciate that frankness in your work. I think it's one of your strengths as a writer that you give yourself permission to include the sorts of things that others might shy away from. I see the theme of personal boundaries running through *The Middle Room* and, in *Imagination Verses*, the words "borders" and "boundaries" often appear. What you're saying about desire and when desire is inappropriate or not seems connected with that.

JM: Yes. I like that you brought up the borders question. *Imagination Verses* was obsessed with borders and boundaries. I'm not sure if I know exactly why. I did grow up on a border: San Diego is on the border with Mexico and I lived in Mexico until I was five. Those two cultures were very much part of my life. So there was a kind of literal border in my life. It's funny because recently there was a poetry job at UC San Diego and I called a friend who had had that job previously and asked if I should apply for it. She said "well, do you do any work on border cultures?" (which is in fashion in academia right now). I said, no, I'm a poet, I do nothing with border cultures! But then I was thinking, I write obsessively about borders, but not in a way the academy would recognize. But I also think my border obsession has to do with my interest in the questions of freedom and responsibility, and social control. I don't know that I'm thinking about this as much anymore, but at the time I was writing *Imagination Verses* this question was central to me.

ST: That's really useful. I see your memoir as an enquiry into how one's sense of boundaries is formed by one's background, one's family relationships and so on.

JM: When I was younger, I didn't understand why people who cared for you needed you to limit yourself in certain ways in order for that care to function properly. I felt like I needed to be totally free. So I had boundary issues. I have friends who, because they have stable boundaries, can travel to exotic places and remain totally themselves. At least that's how it appears to me. But if I go to a new place, I often feel like a chameleon, as if I will change completely to fit the new circumstances. And it was the same with people. Though much less so now, I'm much more closed off now, I've become much more conservative. But my boundaries were very undrawn for quite some time.

So there's that tension, and Rousseau is in there as well, in the guise of his *Confessions*, as a model for the tension between your own self-perception and other people's perceptions of you. Others may see you as precocious, but you might feel like a colander, as if things could just pour through you. I think for a long time when I went into social space I didn't know how to negotiate it. It wasn't that I was shy or anything like that, it was just that I needed to feel that the environment was one in which I was accepted in order to do well. That's psychology—my poems ended up for a long time being this voice of the social self that could not be expressed in social space.

Sometimes I think the lyric tradition, from Sappho forward, is basically a record of that voice. The lyric is a kind of seeping through of things that the culture does not really want to celebrate, while the epic is more of a celebration of the cultural triumphs. I think that's why one finds a lot of inappropriate desire in the lyric tradition, and a lot of uncomfortable whining and self-pity—you know, all of those feelings that there's no real place for, but that most people are experiencing. So the lyric is a document of selfhood as it's being constructed or repressed in society. After all, if you have a very active interior life the question arises, where will that interior life have outlet if there's no room for it in school or in other public places?

ST: Do you experience the decisions you make as a writer as risky, in terms of negotiating those kinds of tensions?

JM: It depends on the book! I mean there's often a moment where I'm just in deep terror after a book is published, because I know that some things, whether formal decisions or some element of the content, are risky. A poet I admire who I think of as taking a lot of such risks is John Wieners. When asked by Raymond Foye if he had a poetics he replied, "I try to write the most embarrassing thing I can think of".[2] For a while now I have been trying to answer the question: what is the difference between this statement, Wieners' "confession"—and he was a Catholic, so confession is a very over-determined word for him—and the confession of confessional poetry? Is there a difference between this kind of poetry and that of Sylvia Plath?

Though most young girl-poets in this country go through a phase where they read Sylvia Plath and want to be her, I never went through that. Yet I admit that a lot of my poems could be read as confessional. This shouldn't be a problem except that the confessional poets were very

---

[2] John Wieners, *Cultural Affairs in Boston: Poetry and Prose 1956–1985* (Santa Rosa, CA: Black Sparrow Press, 1988), p. 15.

much maligned among my circle—the worst thing you could possibly do was to be a confessional poet. Of course, the confessionals were linked to a certain moment of psychoanalysis in this country, the kind of Freudianism that was fashionable among intellectuals in the post-war era. Confessional poetry performs a high dramatic staging of the self and the interior life. Wieners also performs this staging, and yet the way I've often thought of his staging is in terms of camp or torch, like being in drag, a kind of melodrama in which the emotions become a landscape of excess. You know the doll Barbie, do they have Barbie in England? [**ST**: Yes!] As Barbie is to gender, John Wieners' poems are to emotion! Barbie is *echt* gender, there's no woman who looks like her. It's that kind of emotionality.

By contrast, when I read Sylvia Plath, I feel like she uses emotion in order to distance herself from you. Like she's not *actually* exposing herself, but rather saying outrageous things so that you only think about those things. Like she's hiding behind them—at least that's my experience of reading her poems. It's like meeting someone for the first time and they instantly tell you something very intimate about themselves. What are you supposed to do with such information? Sometimes I think such exchanges are very manipulative, because suddenly you feel, you know, like you can't say anything back, you're stuck.

Of course Plath was writing into a very particular and repressive cultural moment. You can't say that about that time I grew up in. In the seventies in California, no-one was repressed. There was the opposite problem. So I doubt I could have ever thought it too radical to "de-repress" society. To me it's much more about framing and what you choose to value. I know with the memoir I've had some people say to me, I think maybe even John Wilkinson said this, that they just found it hilarious that the content and the style were not connected at all, because the content is so low and the style is so high, but I don't think the content is low, I don't think it's unjustifiable content. But then again—it depends on what you value.

ST: Coming back to this comparison you made between Plath's handling of emotion and Wieners', my understanding of how you were describing the effect of reading Plath, or perhaps the way in which she is generally read, is as if there's this passive-aggressive, "here are my wounds, what are you going to do about it?" kind of gesture. Although I agree with you that Plath is writing to some extent against repression, I think that she does nevertheless make you aware of language's role in constructing selfhood as well.

JM: Absolutely. And there's more than one Plath! But I guess I am referring more to the Plath industry, and the way that the idea of confessionalism became reduced, as all ideas do. Even Beat poetry is more complicated, interesting and diverse than the *idea* of Beat poetry, which is just bongo drums and black turtlenecks! I'm aware of all that, but still when you say "confessional poetry", there's a response that's very, at least in the community that I run in, "oh that means x and x is bad".

ST: Yes, I absolutely recognize that. It's something I've been testing in relation to the poetic community that I am part of—that in the logic of my work as I feel it developing is a necessity to explore territory that I wouldn't have otherwise included. That's partly what draws me to your work as a way of thinking through those issues. But in terms of the comparison with Plath, if Wieners is this figure with whom it feels absolutely authentic…

JM: Well, I should clarify because when I say it's like a poetics in drag, I'm saying it's not authentic, it's high artifice, but high artifice in which you're not mocking anyone—you're allowing yourself to be the vector of mockery. There's a touch of masochism to it, but I'm nevertheless drawn to it. I've been drawn to it since I bought my first Billie Holiday record! I feel that there's a way of dealing with embarrassment or extreme emotional response that those territories (drag, camp, etc) cover. The motivation is different. Instead of, "I live in a repressed suburban community and I'm a mother and wife…" it's more like a completely different relationship to culture, a different sense of inappropriateness perhaps.

This whole "what is confessionalism" question is something I started to think about a couple of years ago when I taught a course on Wieners at Naropa. Following that, I taught a course at the University of Maine on Duncan, Wieners and Schuyler called 'A Girlish Possibility', in which tried to think about postwar American gay male poets: gender, masculinity, sexuality, and so on. In both instances I started to wonder, why is this poetry not confessionalism? It's not a question that I've answered satisfactorily for myself. Is it just a difference of communities and anthologies? Or is it open form poetics versus traditional forms? Certainly class and education come into it as well.

ST: Perhaps the way I reflected back the Plath–Wieners comparison made it sound too absolute, but I wonder if the difference is in the attitude to language? Rod Mengham wrote about your work that: "it works to confirm the value of feelings at the same time as it distracts the attention powerfully away from them."[3]

JM: That's just what I was saying about Sylvia Plath!

ST: I suppose it is! Mengham picks up on your line: "I admit I've suffered from a 'parallax of heart'",[4] and uses the figure of parallax to discuss the effect of what he calls displacement or dislocation in your work.

JM: It's an interesting reading. I don't know that I would agree that I try to distract from feelings, but I do believe that, once you write it in a poem, it's artifice, it isn't feelings. The feelings become framed by form, and there is some control and there's some artfulness, hopefully, to it. That said, I absolutely believe that we experience emotions as true, and not as being full with artifice.

When I was younger it wasn't just that I wanted to listen to Billie Holiday, but that Billie Holiday was teaching me how to feel about my own love affairs. And it wasn't a good lesson necessarily, but it was one I enjoyed and started to recognize! So my own sentimental education, so to speak, was influenced by cultural objects, artists, paintings, literature, music. I've noticed this "education" when teaching as well. When students write about love, I discover that they think about love in the ways that the pop culture has taught them to think about it, so they don't know what they're feeling anymore.

Ruskin says that the painter has to learn to see again. I feel that way about feelings. And yet instead of wanting to find some semblance of a "natural emotion" I have always been interested in going *into* the artificially created space of emotionality, and cultivating it. As a result my family thought I was wildly over-emotional and completely sentimental. This made me feel emotionally somewhat like a gay man who hadn't come out yet: why is she acting this way? I think I was just being drawn towards

---

[3] Rod Mengham, 'Reading Jennifer Moxley' in *Parataxis* 10, (2001), 103–108, 106. In this paper, Mengham focuses on Moxley's *Imagination Verses* in the 1996 Tender Buttons edition.
[4] Ibid., p. 103. See also Jennifer Moxley, 'The Waver in the Orbit of Uranus Becomes Unexplainable' in *Imagination Verses* (Great Wilbraham: Salt Publishing, 2003), p. 80.

artifice, because it was more interesting to me.

ST: It's not far from "I is another" isn't it?

JM: No, it isn't actually.

ST: But it also brings to mind how culture is at least partly charged with the responsibility of helping children to recognise emotions and to name them and to know what they consist of. Parenting does that as well, but sometimes fails, or at least can create confusion. Then, of course, what is understood by feelings and emotions, and the differences between them, is culturally and historically determined.

JM: Yes, you're right. What I realized when I was younger was that I wanted my life to be like an opera—always in emotional extremity—which is ridiculous. Now I can just get such feelings out of my system by *going* to the opera. I don't need to live it. Yet I love the permeable boundary art can create. It is the most beautiful thing when you're looking at a work of art, or reading a poem, and you actually lose the boundary between yourself and it and start feeling that you're being spoken to directly. To me, that's an aesthetic experience of the highest order. I went through a long mourning process when I realized life alone can't produce that feeling.

ST: That's fascinating. What does the practice of translation mean to you creatively in this context?

JM: In an interview with Noah Eli Gordon[5] I made the claim that any poet who thinks deeply about language risks entering a mystical zone. It's a very Mallarméan argument. As a bilingual person, I have also noticed that the experience of two languages is enough to make you experience this "zone". As you must know from your learning of Polish, the space *between* languages can feel amazingly precarious. I've been re-reading Duncan lately—I had put him aside for a long time—and he is a great guide through this kind of inquiry. He was always interested in what language might reveal, though he probably would have spoken of the above in terms of "mysteries" and not mysticism, for he thought this latter was about knowledge, which he claimed not to have. Recently, so many great resources to guide us through

---

[5] 'Mysteries: Jennifer Moxley in conversation with Noah Eli Gordon', *Jacket* 37 (Early 2009). Viewable at: http://jacketmagazine.com/37/iv-moxley-ivb-gordon.shtml

his thinking have been made easily available: the Levertov–Duncan letters, and Penn Sound, where one can find sound files of many of Duncan's lectures. He thinks in talk, so he's a real pleasure to listen to.

But back to this question of the mystical, any discussion of which seems to have gone missing in contemporary poetry. The extent to which this is so really struck me when I started reading Devin Johnston's book *Precipitations*. It's not about mysticism per se, but rather about occult practice in Modernism.[6] He writes about H.D., Duncan, James Merrill, Susan Howe and Nathaniel Mackey. He makes the argument that Modernism's interest in Occultism has been ignored in post-war criticism, in which Modernism has been read exclusively as a movement motivated by formal experimentation and innovation. The occult side just becomes an embarrassment, something to be pushed under the rug. Let's pretend that H.D. didn't have visions, or talk to dead RAF pilots! Of course some people are thinking about this aspect of the modernist legacy, but it's definitely not in vogue. I often end up at these questions through my interest in Symbolism, through Rimbaud and Mallarmé, and their way of incorporating these threads of thought through language itself, which is to me one of the most mystical instruments.

ST: I favour the term "transpersonal" as a way to address the mystical. It's about boundaries again: when one experiences a removal of boundaries or limits.

JM: Absolutely, that's what a mystical experience is, boundaries go away and you see the totality. There's the other problem, which is that, in the post-war era and the post-modern era, the word "totality" has very negative connotations. It is only seen as a political term. The thinking has really been focused on statecraft and politics. I have a very limited interest in that. I'm interested in the terms that artists bring to a culture, not those brought by politicians. That's also something that makes me very unlike someone who thinks of him or herself as avant-garde, in so far as the European avant-garde was founded on a politicized anti-art position and associated art with bourgeois culture. I do privilege the artist, and I do not believe that art is inherently bourgeois and indulgent. It's not that I feel that artists are *superior* to other people, no, that's not it, but I do feel that there is something different in what they can see about the culture than

---

[6] *Precipitations: Contemporary American Poetry as Occult Practice* (Middletown, CT: Wesleyan University Press, 2002).

what the politician or the financier sees. All are part of a whole, a totality.

Totality, universalism, all these terms have been demonized because they've been seen only in the political frame. My book *The Line* attempts to think through some of these issues. At least that's one way of reading it. Some took it to be about poetic lineage, which is not what I was thinking about. Then there's the obvious reading, that *The Line* is about the poetic line, but to me the line is an image of connectivity, how language becomes a portal through which we can glimpse the totality. This kind of thinking started when I began to notice the similarity between descriptions of mystical experiences and, for example, the way Mallarmé writes about poetry. There's a similar kind of *trying to account for what's happening*, and in both the human involved sees themself as a vehicle through which something else is being seen or happening. It's not so far from Spicer and Duncan's theories about dictation.

ST: I wanted to talk to you about *The Line* and the ongoing enquiry that's there from the earlier work in terms of time, memory and identity, but also about the politics of postmodernity, which you've just raised. In the afterword to *Often Capital* there are hints of a critique of postmodern theory in references to "some cosmic or historical moment in which it was suddenly decided that subjects so "constructed" could see no difference between right or wrong",[7] and in *The Line*: "the empiricist has written: bipartite divisions are false"[8] and "an obliterative drive to lose self-consciousness in linguistic equations".[9] My own relation to that body of work is both enabling and problematic, but more generally in Britain responses to "theory" are still quite polarized. Growing up as a poet of my generation, theory was part of your equipment and it was extraordinarily useful, up to a point. But then things move on and change and you require other ways of dealing with things. Philosophically now, with writers like Badiou and Rancière, there's a return to the notion of universality, albeit in a different way. I'm wondering how much an awareness of philosophical trends informs what you do?

JM: I think that, similar to what you're describing in Britain, there's a way the word postmodernity or postmodern theory was reduced to a parodic version, in which the American Academy turned the entrance

---

[7] See Jennifer Moxley, *Often Capital* (Chicago: Flood, 2005), p. 57–58.
[8] See Jennifer Moxley, *The Line* (Sausalito: Post-Apollo Press, 2007), p. 19.
[9] Ibid., p. 40.

of that discourse into the destruction of the tradition. I was at Brown in the nineties and people left the English department and started another department because of what they called the "theory wars", which you may have had in the UK. [**ST**: Yes, absolutely.] But I was not part of that. Steve was more involved, he's deeply read in theory, and has way more knowledge about it than I do. But I was in the midst of that environment and I couldn't help but be affected by what was going on. This was partly because the Language Poets, my direct predecessors, embraced a certain kind of theoretical engagement with contemporary thought.

I think we can tie this back to what Barrett said, his distinction between technique and method. Certain kinds of postmodern thought have been embraced through what I would almost call a "narrative of a conversion". Your convert to this thinking, after which you think everything you previously thought was wrong, then you become intolerable to all your friends because you show them how *they* are wrong. You have a structural analysis, they don't. It happens with feminism as with Marxism, anything that structurally challenges your thinking. It doesn't mean that I think such theoretical analyses and critiques are wrong, but rather that often a simplistic and rather bossy and self-righteous replacement stands in for them. But back to your question. I never sat down and said well, I'm going to have a critique of postmodernity (not that I think you're asking me that!). I've never read Badiou or Rancière. I have read a lot of Barthes, but he's kind of an odd man out. I have read Adorno and feel very sympathetic with a lot of his writing. But I'm just as likely to go to a writer like Ruskin as to a contemporary theorist.

Like many people, Marx's critique of capital was my first structuralist revelation, the first time I thought, oh my, structure, it's controlling everything! But of course nuance is key here. You know how gloomy you get when you first realize you are determined? Whether you feel determined by patriarchy or capitalism or whatever, a gloom overtakes you. You ask: how will I live, what can I do?! Sometimes it seems that what then goes wrong is that you start to feel at war, even in peacetime. You get this kind of extreme, martyr, war-like response to it, even if you are privileged, educated, writing poetry, etc. It can be a self-indulgent trap. You start failing to experience what you're experiencing because you're seeing everything through an ideology that's supposedly critiquing ideology, so it's just a trap, a maze.

I feel, again as an artist, to embrace one ideology and just use it as a kind of crib sheet on how to respond to situations is a disaster. I mean, we know it's a disaster, because state-controlled art is horrible. It loses individuality, which is the only thing that we've gained in all these years of so-called "progress". The free life of the mind, the true individual, is always at risk, so to just throw it out the window because you've figured out that some things are determined seems to me a mistake. I still believe that the individual can be self-determined at some level within the structures. At the same time, when it comes to language, all this goes out the window, although I don't feel that language itself is state-controlled, which was the ideological stance (in terms of the way it was transmitted) the Language Poets took. They believed that poets disrupted that control, by showing you how it really was. Of course, that's a gross oversimplification.

There is a sort of pedagogy that goes along with this that drives me crazy though. The idea that poetry is going to teach you how to be free, the rhetoric about liberating the reader from their own oppression, the oppression of believing the texts they read. Last summer I was a visiting poet for a week in a MFA program. The students there were very hip, very savvy—and they wanted to be theoretical. I sat down with maybe twelve different students: I read their work ahead of time and then we met one-on-one. If I asked, "well, what are you trying to do with this poem?" ninety percent of them said something akin to "I'm trying to teach the reader, liberate the reader from their delusions". It was as if it had…

ST: Become an orthodoxy?

JM: Yeah, it was bizarre. I was thinking, well, who is this reader? Can you find me a reader of poetry first of all?! It just seemed like it had become an orthodoxy that had no meaning anymore, and if you pressured it a bit it was crumbly and meaningless. Maybe, I wondered, now that there aren't any readers, this is a collective dream.

ST: We've got more poets than readers.

JM: Exactly! Maybe that's why it's so attractive, because if you keep saying the word "reader" over and over again maybe you'll conjure one up.

ST: One day they'll appear!

JM: I'm not going to generalize, but a lot of that work is actually very ungenerous to readers. It refuses to risk something, to build its own structure, so this thing that's supposedly there to help a reader is actually often a frustration to a reader.

ST: I recognize that. It's interesting to think that it's still going on, so long after the first era of theory. I'm guilty of it myself in a sense that my teaching does involve some of those texts, but I want to use them in such a way that they're enabling.

JM: Theoretical texts? I just taught Foucault last Spring in my graduate class.

ST: To writers?

JM: Well, it was a literature class, but I always have some writers in my courses. It was a course on American Modernism. I wasn't bringing Foucault in to mock him or say he's wrong or to say this is the truth, it was simply that he offered a useful frame. It's like that with many theoretical structures. I guess what I'm awkwardly trying to say is that I'm not hostile to postmodernism, that's not my position, but neither do I embrace all its terms equally, or find it describes every current dilemma.

When I was at Brown I hung out with the poets on one hand, some of who were anti-theory, and Steve's set of PhD student friends on the other hand, all of whom were theory heads who wouldn't go to a poetry reading or read a contemporary poem to save their life! I believe that being in the middle of these two groups allowed me to see the strengths and limitations of both. In both cases I try to resist settling on a dogma, picking an ideological stance and running with it. It just doesn't strike me as a very interesting artistic or intellectual position. I make aesthetic judgements. I might argue that one poet is shit, and another great, but not along camp lines. I don't want to make a wholesale rejection of any one moment or movement.

ST: Perhaps the most productive movements are formed among writers with distinct differences, otherwise you wind up with people just reinforcing each other in the same practices. I think Language Poetry was so dynamic for so long because people were in dialogue across very different lines, and they found a space that gave everybody permission. I think another way of conducting this interview project would have been to get everybody in the same room somehow, as the Language Poets used to do.

JM: A lot of it's just also the fact of a cultural change, which is that artists cannot move to big cities en masse and live cheaply like they could in the sixties and seventies.

Talking Poetics

ST: As I learned in Manhattan—how all the artists were priced out of existence there.

JM: And the same with San Francisco. Young people in particular can't, and that's when it happens, that's when those group dynamics are so generative. I think that has a lot to do with it, the sense of geography. One thing that some MFA programs have done is to provide that little space where young people can all get together and not have to think only about paying their rent for two years. Then you might have something happen.

ST: We were talking earlier about confessional poetry and the overlap with your own practice. The difference might be to do with the attitude towards language but is it also just because of where you've come from in terms of your journey in writing? Perhaps these stylistic affiliations cloud the issue of encountering each writer in their difference?

JM: I think in some ways the decision to embrace a certain aesthetic trend or tradition is just to narrow the reading list. First, it's who do you fall in love with? If for me it was Rimbaud, a lot followed from that. But not everything, so you get to edit out what doesn't. We don't have time to read it all, right? So in some ways I feel like it's chance, it's happenstance: what book you come into contact with that turns you on when you're first starting and where that book leads you. You build your raft very slowly. So partly it's just a narrowing of the reading list and then when you're older, you're like, oh, maybe I have time to go back and read Eleanor Wiley.

ST: It's almost like you're being imprinted isn't it?

JM: Yes, you're finding your taste, your aesthetic values, and then you're finding that it's not casual and that there's an argument about it. To me that's important. I like to argue about aesthetic values. I don't want *everything* to be good! So there's a narrowing. The second issue for me is the importance, in the tradition that I consider myself a part of, of the way the work comes into the world. The reproduction of the work in the world has always been connected to a living community that you're in dialogue with—the small presses—and an eschewing of that system that pretends there is a kind of universal value that can just be seen: the whole prize structure and the way mainstream publishing promotes poetry. So that's extremely important to me in terms of the way that my work is read. I want the bringing of the work into the world to have meaning, not to be an alienated experience, and for my readers not to be alienated either. You know, you're a reader of mine and we're sitting talking, it's not alienated.

ST: It feels quite natural in a way.

JM: Yes. I feel that the tradition from Ezra Pound, well, from Rimbaud forward, and in Whitman, has this sense that you make it from the ground up. Then it's a dialogue and a process. Those are two things that are very important to me. I think my work is completely understandable if you think of it as coming out of Modernism and the New American Poetry. If you erase that history and forget that, for example, Barrett Watten was very much involved in Olson, or that Silliman would not be possible without Williams, then you're missing a part of the story. But if you think, oh, ok, Oppen, Williams, then the Language Poets, then the work seems more grounded. Then you add in the Francophone influence, which you can also get through Wallace Stevens and Michael Palmer, who have also been very important to me and have another way of paying attention to language and form and pressuring the poem. It's a poetry that naturally evolves from what preceded it.

Williams tried to change what a poem was, he was in deep dialogue with the historical circumstance and the linguistic circumstance that he felt needed to be thought about. I feel that when someone just accepts the change in what a poem is without feeling that from deep within, that there's a problem. Sometimes I've been reviewed in such a way where it seems like the person is trying to figure out how I am critiquing or using artifice in a way that's similar to xyz. It's not seeing the forest for the trees. It's as if they think she can't be serious about the lyric part so we'll just look at this other part and say that she's just mocking the lyric part. There's this funny inability to read the work because of where it's coming from. But if you think about the history in a longer sense, this work should be readable.

I've always insisted that I won't accept the version of a poet that is the canonized, conservative version. So to me Shelley, for example, is so radical. It's in part because of my education. I was never really taught this stuff in school so I could always accept it the way I wanted to. I feel more of a kinship to a poet of the past, than a sense that, oh that's my great-grandfather's tradition, so I want to kill it and create my own tradition. I also think that there is a feminist issue here because I feel that, in the Western world, as soon as women started to be enfranchised and able to have selves, then it became unfashionable. So I feel like that's not a good deal!

ST: I'd agree with that!

JM: In your written questions you asked about the link between *Sleep's Powers* and *The Line* and I just wanted to correct an impression, because I wrote *The Line* before I translated *Sleep's Powers*, so the Risset could not possibly have influenced it. But I could see how those two books could seem connected. It is fascinating to me that after I wrote *The Line* and published it, I then turned to translating a book about sleep in which a similar thinking through of that threshold between sleeping and waking had been explored. Perhaps, because I'd thought a lot about sleep and waking when I was writing *The Line*, I went to the shelves to translate something and I picked up the Risset. After I translated *Sleep's Powers*, I got so fascinated with the short essay form, that I turned to writing my own book of short essays. This work is directly influenced by *Sleep's Powers*, and when I finish it I'll write an introduction to that effect. So Risset's book has influenced me, but in this other direction, toward attempting essays that move freely between personal memories and reflections to literary observations to philosophical questions.

ST: It's something Barthes does beautifully as well, isn't it?

JM: Exactly. I had a revelation after translating Risset, it was that a really good essay is one in which, while reading it, you start to write your own essay. Unlike the academic article, which generally tries to survey all of the things that have been said before and add something new, holes in essays are enabling. Risset has a memory and then a thought and you correspondingly start having your own memory and thought, so it becomes this true way of the reader creating their own work.

Jeffrey C. Robinson, a Romanticist, wrote a charming little book called *The Walk: Notes on a Romantic Image*.[10] It's a book of short essays on walking in Romantic poetry, but he also reflects on his own relationship to walking and talks about the foot and the stride. In his introduction he says that when he was writing the book, everyone he told about it had stories: oh, you have to include this poem and this walk! People could not stop thinking of examples! That's how it felt translating Risset. I kept

---

[10] Jeffrey C. Robinson, *The Walk: Notes on a Romantic Image* (Illinois: Dalkey Archive, 2006). As Robinson puts it: "No one has ever engaged me on the subject of walking literature who has not offered an instance that "simply can't be left out". Instead, let me offer you the occasion to start producing your own instances and memories and perhaps even the writing desire...", p. 5.

thinking, why didn't she write about sleep in this particular book, or about that image of sleep? I realized I had been thinking about these omissions as a negative, as if she had forgot this and that, but in actual fact it was a positive, because she allowed me to think of all these things, all these examples. It's a beautiful gift. So that's what I'm trying to do, but my book is going to be on things, material things. It's a completely different topic, but something that matters to me.

ST: There's a striking remark in *The Middle Room* about how comfort can derive from material things: "how the simple company of one's favorite things [...] *real material things*—affirms your identity and sense of safety".[11]

JM: Yes, that's what I'm writing about. I'm trying to go against Plato! I'm against that whole degradation since Plato—and in Christianity for that matter, which has failed to keep things out of it—of the material existence in favour of the spiritual existence. The argument I want to make—and obviously I'm not the first one to make it—is that it is through the material world that the spiritual world is manifest. It's an optimist-gnosis. Like Gerard Manley Hopkins's sense of instress, the idea that—I always confuse inscape and instress, so apologies if that's happening now—the world has a divine signature and that it's not in the degradation of the thing but in the adoration of the thing that the divine is reached.

ST: There's that notion that Hopkins gets from Duns Scotus as well, *haecceitas*.

JM: Yes. When I started looking into this, there are a lot of thinkers who have considered it, even the Surrealists with their idea that you can see labour in objects and Marx's idea of the commodity as magical.

ST: De Certeau talks about it as well, objects take on a kind of aura of their use.[12] I've a line in *Momentum*: "objects change / into spiritual / matter"!

JM: So you're right with me! Just as the word "totality" got reduced to a

---

[11] See Jennifer Moxley, *The Middle Room* (Berkeley, CA: Subpress, 2007), p. 599.
[12] "The display includes innumerable familiar objects, polished, deformed, or made more beautiful by long use; everywhere there are as well the marks of active hands and laboring or patient bodies for which these things composed the daily circuits, the fascinating presence of absences whose traces were everywhere". Michel de Certeau, *The Practice of Everyday Life* (Berkeley and London: University of California Press, 1984), p. 21.

political meaning, I feel like the idea of the object has had a very limited sense of referring only to commodity culture, only to the products that are selling on the market.

ST: In the interview I did with John Wilkinson he spoke about John Wieners' fascination, as he saw it, with the consuming world: that he didn't shut it out but investigated it.[13]

JM: I can totally see that in his work. The term that we have not talked about, which is behind all of this, is imagination. What's fascinating to me is the way that, when you're a child, an object might not have any real value in the world, but can become the total focus of an imaginative world. Most writers I know are fetishists about their tools, and they're comfortable talking about their relationship to a pen or a certain notebook, but they wouldn't call themselves interested in consumer culture. So I'm interested in the way that the imagination is connected up to the object world, almost to the point of endowing it with personality.

To aid my research I just ordered *The Comfort of Things* by the British anthropologist Daniel Miller.[14] He did a sociological study of one street in London and looked at people's different relationships to the objects in their homes. Miller's trying to think about how objects create memory and history. We have this assumption that if you surround yourself with things, you won't have relationships with people. He's making the exact opposite argument—he says that people who value things also value people, and people who value and care for things, including things from the past, tend to have a more social life and sense of value for humans. So valuing things does not take the place of the valuing of people.

ST: I suppose one would have to be careful not to use that as a justification for the sort of consumerism that can actually be harmful as well [**JM**: Well, this is the risk, you have to frame it.], because I think that people do perhaps use consuming as a way of satisfying needs that are not being met in other ways.

---

[13] "[Wieners'] relationship with popular culture is something which is important to him—and with American capitalist and consumerist society—in that his work fully acknowledged the absolute allure of that and at the same time registered the degradations of it on his own body and on his experience and his social experience". John Wilkinson and Scott Thurston, 'Fascination and Effacement: an Interview', *Poetry Salzburg Review* 4 (Spring 2003), 19-20.
[14] Daniel Miller, *The Comfort of Things* (Cambridge: Polity, 2008).

JM: Absolutely, but he's making a more subtle argument. It's going against that residue of Christian moralism that any kind of materialism is crass. Obviously there is a very big difference between the person who has three hundred thousand dollars of credit card debt because they can't stop buying things, and the person who understands how to value the material world around them.

ST: Yes, there's a whole poetics of it, isn't there? It's very interesting to open that area.

JM: In addition to Risset, I have also been influenced by Barthes. I listened to his series of lectures at the *Collège de France* called 'Comment vivre ensemble'.[15] He organizes his thinking into what he calls "dossiers". Every time he introduces a new topic or theme, he says "I'm going to open a dossier". So I decided to write my book that way. I open a file and follow a thread, which usually consists of three or four essays on, say, dishes, or clothes, or objects in novels, or poems and so on. Now the problem is how to put it all together, but I'll solve that when the writing is done.

ST: I'd like to ask you about the creative process of writing *The Middle Room*—its challenges, whether it affected your poetry writing, and also whether you would write another volume in the future.

JM: *The Middle Room* was extremely difficult to write. I started in about '96 or '97 but very cursorily, I didn't commit. I just started writing down some memories. I didn't really take it that seriously 'til we got to Paris. I had probably written a hundred pages before then, but it was very rough and I hadn't found the voice or the style or the focus. The biggest challenge for me was how to create a structure that had a kind of sequence or logic to it. And also how to write a sentence! Sometimes I think I became a poet because I was more comfortable leaping from one thing to the next and allowing associations to develop than in making coherent structures. And I had (and continue to have) so much trouble with grammar. So in some ways I feel like writing *The Middle Room* was basically an apprenticeship to the sentence. I still made errors, but I worked really hard at it.

I probably came home from France with about three hundred completed pages, but even many of those got completely revised. In the first three or four years here in Maine, in the summers when I wasn't working, I really wrote and revised a lot. The first three or four chapters have the most

---

[15] Available online at UBU Web: http://www.ubu.com/sound/barthes.html

layers—like an archaeological dig—the drafting process is twelve drafts down. They were the least fluid. But, from chapter ten forward I wrote very quickly. It was as though I was wandering around for a very long time and then suddenly I found a path. After that it was easy and I could just churn pages out.

I did a great deal of research. I went through my journals and Steve's journals, I went through old letters. I asked friends who I'd corresponded with to send my letters back so that I could see what I was saying about my life at that time. I looked at photographs, I looked at cheque book registers and bills. I did research on my own life, as though I was writing the biography of another person. What gradually emerged was this character of my younger self who became very artificial in a way. Her voice took over. She became like a fictional character. I'm not saying she does anything in the book that I didn't do—she owns the cars I owned, she dates the boys I dated—but in many ways she became this literary device apart.

I really feel that the work of writing this book was an act of self-psychoanalysis. By the end of it certain, I don't want to say symptoms, but certain emotional difficulties in my life vanished, because I addressed some things and I rethought what happened. There was so much change in my life so quickly when I was younger.

Writing *The Middle Room* had a profound effect on my poetry. You can probably see a thread from *Imagination Verses* to *The Sense Record*, but *The Sense Record* was written during the process of writing *The Middle Room* and you might notice that the lines get a lot longer, the syntax gets more entangled and complex, and there's more narrative thrust than in *Imagination Verses*. In some ways *The Line*, which is the next book I wrote after *The Sense Record*, was an attempt to go back to leaving things out and to a kind of pared-down style. Can I write something without complexity? Can I make a simple formal linguistic surface that is at the same time complicated in what it is saying but isn't using more words in order to be complicated? I just wanted to have a different kind of artifice, a less ornate artifice, to go back to that simplicity.

The Line was also written after a return to Rimbaud and Baudelaire, after a re-reading of the prose poem tradition. With a few exceptions, I'd been unhappy about contemporary prose poetry because I thought the prose poem should have something driving it that is similar to what drives a poem in lines. When I went back to Baudelaire and Rimbaud I realized how much they had taken from prose: they were telling stories, using hypotaxis and so on. That was where I started from when I wrote *The Line*.

To go back to *The Middle Room*, I actually felt that I was being influenced by too ornate a style. But then I started reading—and this is going to sound funny—Noël Coward's memoirs, and he helped me become more direct, and feel that it was okay to sometimes say: months passed, period! Steve thought he was my little genius of taking away the ornate style that I had. Well, perhaps not taking it away, but calming it down. It was much less calm than even now, it was outrageously excessive! The artifice, the style that I developed, I don't think of as archaic as some people have said.

ST: In *The Middle Room*?

JM: Yeah. You're British so you probably have a different response. I've found that my work has been received in Britain very differently than in America. Here there's a kind of response where people say oh, this is so old-fashioned or Victorian or ornate or baroque. I think what they mean is, it sounds like literature.

ST: Because you use metaphors?

JM: Yes. And, with some exceptions, because my work doesn't often attempt to imitate spoken speech. In the tradition that I'm in, driven by Williams's ideas about poetry needing to be written with an American cadence and so on, there's a great suspicion of anything that sounds like Britishness or literariness: the whole T. S. Eliot is bad, Williams is good thing. Even among highly-educated, highly literary people, they want to sound regular and pared-down, without metaphor, like Spicer.

ST: Objectivist in a way?

JM: I guess so. There's a resistance to seeing "speech" as its own form of artifice, there's a sense that it's natural and real. But that's another topic! You asked if I was going to write another memoir to follow *The Middle Room*. My original plan was to treat *The Middle Room* as the first volume in a two-volume series. The second volume was going to begin with the death of my friend Helena (the dedicatee of the book), eight months after my mother's death. The back story is that, originally, I began this entire memoir project in order to write about Helena's death, but when I got to the end of the narrative arc, I realized there was no way to do it, there was no way to write about Helena's death that wouldn't feel added on. The plan was to write another volume, to start there and end with the publication of *Imagination Verses*—in effect, the end of my apprenticeship. But at present I've abandoned this plan. It's too much grief, too exhausting.

Writing *The Middle Room* did change my poetry and I feel like it helped me grow up as a poet in some ways, to become a more diligent craftsperson, and not always hide behind the fact that if I couldn't deal with how to say something I could just leave it out or imply it. The thing about contemporary gestures or free verse is that there's a way you can be lazy and just evoke things.

ST: And dodge things at the same time.

JM: Yes. I started to notice this in reading some of the more complex poets, like Hopkins for example. Open field poetics often permits a different way of thinking to emerge, and sometimes a thinking-through, but the attenuation of that gesture has created, to my mind, poetry with gaps. I wanted to fill in those blanks a little bit, and I think doing the memoir was a sort of apprenticeship in that.

ST: It's also interesting that, after *The Line*, *Clampdown* seems to be coming full-circle in that there are poetic versions of some of the stories in *The Middle Room*. It reminds me of poems in *The Sense Record* also.

JM: I see it as more a *Sense Record*-like book in that it's a collection of lyrics. But *The Line* was a necessary palate-cleanser after *The Middle Room* and it allowed me to work out some issues I was having around memory. In *Clampdown*, some of those poems were written before, during and after *The Line*, so I was still writing lyrics while I did this serial work. But *The Line* was written in a small amount of time—maybe three months—and I really did get up every morning and write a poem. It became a more meditative practice, rather than poem by poem. I really did write it when I was barely awake. I would get out of bed early, make a coffee and then go to my office. I can't remember if I would look at what I had done the day before, but I would just try to stay in the state that I had awoken in.

I wrote *The Line* in winter and when I was mourning for the end of *The Middle Room*. I had been desperate to finish it, but when I did, I felt bereft, in part I think because while writing it I felt like I was with my lost friends and family again. When I finished, it felt like they were in a little coffin and I had buried them! It was horrible in a way. I started getting angry at the book and feeling it was replacing my memory, that it had become my memory.

I was also having very intense and emotional dreams while writing *The Line*, and sort of out of body events, the feeling of being in a space that was neither in memory nor the present. I think it was partly because I didn't know where to locate myself once *The Middle Room* was over. It took me a long time to feel located in my life here in Maine frankly, because I had this sense that we were only here temporarily. And I felt out of place in my academic job, for lots of complicated reasons. There's a lot of anger in the *The Line* about my academic job. I don't know if that comes out at all?!

ST: Yes, I can think of a few moments! I also read 'The Milky Way' very much as a description of an out of body experience.[16]

JM: I had a few like that in the early mornings. It's also in 'Possessed' where I get lifted up from the table and taken through the roof.[17]

ST: By the albatross?!

JM: Yeah! I think that it was written in a state of feeling without a space, without a place, without a grounding. I was also trying to confront my own fear of, for lack of a better word, the void, which I have always associated with sleep. But during this time I started to try and think about sleep as a creative space, like the Surrealists did I suppose, but with a difference. I started taking some of the images out of my sleep and using them for the poem. Many people write from dreams, but I had only done it periodically and never systematically. I was interested in oblivion, which I fear.

So *The Line* was coming out of some of these issues, and going back to Rimbaud, and thinking about mystical experience and string theory. When I was reading about different mystical experiences—Julian of Norwich, for example—I started to think about how a lot of what the mystics were describing was not only connected to language and creativity but also to the scientific idea that the universe is all connected together. So those were some of the touch points.

I realized that this was also a return to a desire to think about my own sense of void from the point of view of my own longing for something spiritual, my own longing for the divine, which I could not express through

---

[16] See Jennifer Moxley, *The Line* (Sausalito, CA: The Post-Apollo Press, 2007), p. 22.
[17] Ibid., p. 41.

traditional means. I felt unlettered in that way. I don't know how to speak the language of organized religion because I wasn't raised learning it. Whenever I've confronted it I've always felt profoundly awkward, and also profoundly disappointed with the banality of it. So I was more interested in how the literary accounts of that kind of meaning had expressed, or recognized, feelings that I'd had. *The Line* was trying to think about that, because it was also at the time when I was trying to confront the fact that this is it, it ends with me and no children. I started to believe that if you have children it just distracts you from death.

ST: Could we look closer at 'The Railing'? I was fascinated by this figure of the line that appears in the poem 'The Line' as something which "extends backwards eternally into the past and forward into the future"[18] and then you've got this figure of the railing and the reference to the "missing line" which "suddenly reappears".[19]

JM: It becomes something you can hold on to, like a railing.

ST: Yes. I found that quite a striking image—as a railing which supports but also railing as in to rail against something.

JM: *The Line* is very much concerned with the way that writing replaces you. In 'The Railing' the character—because there is a kind of strange narrative in this text, a kind of an arc—instead of feeling resentment toward the act of writing, the Mallarméan position, begins to feel that writing is a way to travel outside of the limits of corporeality and the material world, as well as something she can trust as a support. So if it's "letter-built"—the railing, the line—and "word-bent" then it suddenly becomes a space in which to live.[20]

During this time I was starting to realize that I preferred to be writing than to be doing other things. It took me so long to actually commit to writing. I wanted to be a writer but when I was writing it was so hard I would rather go out and have a beer! So it wasn't as if I just loved writing, I struggled to be in that space. I wanted it to end so I could show the product. Now it's completely turned around, and I'd rather be in the space and the product is the least interesting part to me. So I was interested in that space, both in the sense of my own writing and the sense of being in literary

---

[18] Ibid., p. 17.
[19] Ibid., p. 48.
[20] Ibid., p. 48.

texts as a reader—this revelation was happening simultaneously—which is where I was thinking that quotidian life had a banality that literature would take away from me: I would go into a textual space. I was also interested in the way texts connect the centuries. It's not an earth-shattering revelation, but perhaps it's been a bit lost of late because of all the rhetoric about how we're supposed to be reading things that reflect back our own identities. That has never been my experience of literature. What was fascinating to me was that I could feel connected to someone who was so historically different. I should have nothing in common with Augustine for example, and actually do not, but I can still find great meaning in his *Confessions*. In his meditation on memory he asks what is memory and where is it and how do you know it? He writes of not remembering babyhood, but because his parents told him things he thinks he remembers it, therefore he asks, was memory *put in* me? When I write "a firm hold on the railing collapses the walls of the tunnel",[21] I think of the tunnel as the trap of the daily, the material, this sense that you're limited by this world. So then suddenly you're outside of it in a much larger space, which is beyond this world.

ST: It leads you to conclude later on in 'The New Constant' that: "With death-bed pressure the every day keeps memory as a form of compassion, the future as unexplored utterance. Between these two perspectives, the line continues to run".[22] It's almost as if the line is keeping those things at bay, or at least providing an alternative route.

JM: Yes, but I didn't set out a plan. With *The Middle Room* I had a chart: this'll happen and then that'll happen, but the concept of the line just emerged. I wanted to ask, if you have no sense that there is a logic or a system, or a force or a consciousness outside of your own—if you come to an existentialist position, in essence—then what? Some would say well, then you live as though that's it, in the moment. And this was something I wasn't interested in accepting. I have always had this sense that there is something beyond my senses, and yet they're the vehicle—the sense record—through which one can get a glimmer or hint of this beyond. So I think in this work, the line emerged as this thing beyond the individual, beyond the self, beyond the moment, and it became perceptible through these metaphors of time and memory. It's a very literal, materialistic

---

[21] Ibid., p. 48.
[22] Ibid., p. 54.

metaphor in a way—to think of a line—but if you think of the way a scientist might talk about the fabric of the universe or the way things are connected, for me there's a great deal of comfort in that, to reject an atomized version of the world.

ST: I made a connection with the sense record in 'The Cover-Up': "records of events your senses stored without your knowledge".[23] In the same poem, does the sentence: "nodules of time transformed into distinct patterns of feeling which, without the intervention of their long lost origins, will remain unchanged"[24] connect to Proust?

JM: Yes, it's a direct description of Proust's *mémoire involontaire*.

ST: I was also thinking of Bergson and Wordsworth. Bergson doesn't believe in time existing in itself but that we occupy what he calls *durées* or durations. "Nodules of time" seemed to be a version of that, but it also resembles Wordsworth's "spots of time". I see a lot of Wordsworth in Proust.

JM: Absolutely. I do think that Wordsworth is a great thinker about time, and about memory as well. The "records of events your senses stored without your knowledge", is the Proust touch-point in so far as in his theory or idea of *mémoire involontaire* there's this revelation of not having remembered what you suddenly remember, not consciously. Walter Benjamin talks about it in his essay on Baudelaire and makes the fascinating claim that the lyric poem can be the catalyst for these kinds of memories.[25]

There's also the sense that, coming out of Freud, every moment you're alive your senses are taking in so much information that you can't consciously process it all. You could spend a lifetime processing whatever happened between the ages of zero and three months if you could remember it. It's obviously there but—and we always use computer metaphors now—you can't access it. Your software gets updated and you can no longer open those files. I can't help thinking that the conscious processing of our experience is quite impoverished when compared to our experience. And I can't help but

---

[23] Ibid., p. 36.
[24] Ibid., p. 36.
[25] Translating the involuntary memory as a form of shock (via Freud) Benjamin explores "how lyric poetry can have as its basis an experience for which the shock experience has become the norm". Walter Benjamin, 'On Some Motifs in Baudelaire' in *Illuminations* (London: Fontana, 1992), p. 158.

get the feeling that Proust got into an obsessive relationship with that, and that he would have never stopped writing his book if he could have lived on, because every node, every moment of experience could be thousands of pages of prose, if you really tried to think it through. So in some ways *The Line* was an attempt to understand but reject that possibility.

ST: I wonder if this speaks back to 'The Railing': "The static textual object animates more unstable movement, creates an immaterial temporality to quell the solitude of your sealed mind".[26]

JM: Yes, I think so, because when you go into a text, when you're reading a book, the narrative therein contained creates a space in which you can live without that rush of information your own life produces, it's a soothing pleasurable space. It also gives you the illusion that you can make sense of things. You know how whenever you attempt to write down what you're experiencing or thinking or believing, there's this great sense of loss that follows regarding what you *can't* record, what you won't have time to record? One thing that interests me about literature is how it can relieve that sense of loss, albeit through an illusion. A work can be complete. Not a work that you write but a work that you read; I think when you write there is different relationship to this feeling altogether. It's dissatisfying to talk about this kind of thing on some level because a lot of it exists as a "feeling" that you get when writing or reading but that is nevertheless very difficult to describe.

ST: There's a poem about loss in *Clampdown* which discusses that experience of writing against the clock. It's in 'The Measure': "Each unconsidered day we live is lost. / I should record the moments as they come / though marking time is seldom worth the cost. / Loss is our lot".[27]

JM: If you look at the final lines of the final poem, you'll see it is a theme in *Clampdown*. It ends: "in knowing knowledge the soul's sole sustenance / and knowing all knowledge must be undone".[28] So the book is also concerned about the quest for something so hard to keep. I've been thinking about this lately because of some older friends, very learned people, who are starting to experience this kind of loss in a very real way—memory loss—not Alzheimer's or anything like that, just run of the mill memory

---

[26] Moxley, *The Line*, p. 48.
[27] See Jennifer Moxley, *Clampdown* (Chicago: Flood Editions, 2009), p. 27.
[28] Ibid., p. 87.

loss. I started thinking about how you spend all of your life—if you are a writer and intellectual—trying to acquire knowledge and then it just starts being erased, literally; you can't remember names or words or books that you've read. We've all experienced this. I've picked up books and said, oh I have always wanted to read this, opened it and found it annotated by my own hand!

So there's a literal way that this happens and there's also the sense that, even if you're not experiencing memory loss *per se*, you don't necessarily have everything to hand that you've accumulated. Just as when we go to write an essay or article we bring in the books that are touch-points and we have to review, we can't just bring that knowledge up from nowhere.

ST: And often it can be different when you do that anyway, because your thinking may have moved on.

JM: And you've also revised: I may have revised Augustine for all I know! Steve has this mode where he just returns to the same books over and over again, so he keeps re-reading Proust, for example. It seems almost French to me for some reason. It's a different way to be a scholar: instead of saying I need to read all these things I haven't read, to say I'm just going to stick with these few books, they are going to be my touchstones.

ST: I think that's my temperament to a degree.

JM: I realize I have a few books like that, *Confessions* is one of them. It is interesting to take a book and read it periodically throughout your life and see how it changes for you and how your memories of it change. So even with my own work, sometimes I look back at it and it looks back at me from a great distance. At other times I'm very close to it. I think that's common.

ST: One of the signs that is hanging over my research in terms of the rationale behind the writers that I'm putting together is this notion of innovation, which is for me tangled up with the tradition that is referred to as "linguistically innovative" in the UK. The way I've chosen to explore it is in the question of what is at stake in that concept now for writing: what's the function of innovation in your work and how do you see it more broadly in terms of contemporary writing?

JM: I think that Steve has prejudiced me against that term "linguistically innovative" because he thinks it's conceptually incorrect, but if it's a current term in critical thinking about this kind of poetry in England, then it makes sense to use it. But I never, just to be totally honest, think about innovation as a useful descriptor of what I'm trying to do. Early on I was introduced to poets that were self-identified as continuing in a tradition of the avant-garde—and I think the Language Poets very consciously adopted that rhetoric—but many critics have questioned whether the word avant-garde has ever been relevant in the United States. If it's more the European avant-garde, it's connected to a certain kind of class structure or notion of the bourgeoisie that just doesn't really function in the United States. Not that we don't have a middle class, but we don't have a middle class in the sense of people who define what's culturally acceptable, so it's a very shaky term in this culture.

When I think about the meaning of the avant-garde in this country, I think of modernism, and I would identify poets who are not trying to disrupt any codified sense of the art, but poets who are trying to go back. It's more of a Wordsworthian tradition. I doubt that Pound or Williams would admit to that, but I see it starting with Wordsworth: the sense that the primary goal of the contemporary poet is to give a true account of the living language and not just use the language that was in the library. That particular gesture started with Wordsworth, and Coleridge, and is explicitly stated so by them. It's also connected to this moment Raymond Williams discusses—in his writing on Romanticism—where the poet starts to feel on the borders of mainstream culture because of the industrial revolution and the sense of what starts to be valued in the culture as a whole.

Poetic identity since Romanticism has been in a contrary relationship to centralised power. The poet has become an exile, outside of the culture, feeling rejected by it and speaking back to it as a rejected voice. Although the mainstream modernists—Pound, Stein, Eliot and Williams—had different relationships to that and some were more centralised than others, there was that continuation of a sense that poetry had to speak the living language.

That's not exactly like avant-gardism, in the sense of an organised movement—an anti-bourgeois movement or anti-art movement—but it's more the legacy I feel connected to. It could be seen as innovative in so far as that whatever you are trying to express will never have been expressed before in that you have never lived before and this moment has never existed before. I feel very calm about this topic because I feel that I can't help but be different, so I try not to worry about it. I've seen people get fairly bogged down with the idea that they have to invent something new formally, but I feel like I don't really care.

I'm fine with writing in more traditional modes and referring to poets of the past and I feel very connected to the idea of tradition—it's very, very important to me. Innovation is less so, the whole "make it new". I don't think I need to worry too much about that, even though there is an economy of poetry going on about me that is judging things as new or not new. You are either producing something that looks like poetry should, according to the moment—which may value newness above all—or you are producing something else.

It's like this difference between influence and imitation: are you influenced by someone or are you imitating someone? I'm hoping that when people read my work they can see that I have read Wordsworth, though I'm not imitating him. He has *influenced* me. Before we've read enough, we often don't hear those echoes. They emerge later, and add new dimension to the work. The picture starts to fill-in in a different way. Robert Duncan calls it being derivative. He's fond of proudly proclaiming: "I am a derivative poet!" He sees himself as a poet who is in dialogue with the tradition, and derives their sources and energy and meaning from that conversation with the past. I feel a very great kinship with that sentiment.

There is a trend, an anti-intellectualism, that comes out of experience-based ideas of poetry and the erasure of the fact that people like Jack Kerouac actually read Proust—you erase that and say "oh no, he just drove". I've actually had students who have said to me: "I don't want to read any other poems because I don't want to get contaminated". [**ST**: That's familiar!] Because I have this authentic voice that I'm just somehow born with. Another thing that fascinates me is the way that students who have never read or even heard of *The New American Poetry* write New American poems, poems that wouldn't have been possible without *The New American Poetry*. It makes me think, that must be just the way poetry sounds now. Hopefully my work will add a voice to that conversation, and allow for some older sounds to come back into the mix. I remember when I read in San Francisco a few years ago, Bob Grenier came up to me afterwards and said, "I thought we weren't allowed to do that anymore!"

ST: I had a similar reaction reading some of the poems in *Hold* in London two or three years ago! This is partly where my interest in your work comes from—its permission for things I've also been trying to negotiate in terms of not wanting to continue in a particular "innovative" vein that I didn't feel served my needs anymore. I wanted to allow other things in, or back in even, so that necessitated a broadening of voice and a picking up of rhetorical strategies that might otherwise be considered beyond the pale, among some of my peers at least.

JM: Duncan tells a great anecdote about giving a reading in which he uses a word—I think it's the word "lovely" or it might be "flowers"—and after the reading Allen Ginsberg comes up to him and says "you can't use that word anymore". And Duncan's like, I hate no, I'm against no, I don't want anything to be not allowed as a poet, as an artist. Then he says, "I fought all my life to be able to say 'fuck' in a poem, and now if I want to say 'lovely', godammit, I'm gonna say 'lovely'!" It's just this moment where Ginsberg—who's supposedly fought his own battles against censorship—comes up and censors Duncan. I've always been interested in the way that a kind of policing of poetic gestures in the name of innovation or freedom is very contradictory. I would rather someone come up and say I don't value that, or I don't think it's aesthetically valid, and have an argument with me than say that's not allowed or that is completely forbidden. It just doesn't make sense to me. If you're supposedly into breaking down boundaries then you should celebrate when others do. That's my relationship to innovation.

ST: It's a term that I feel has become almost unusable really. I'm still invested in it, but I have quite an ambivalent relationship to it. I think it has a very straightforward use value in pointing at certain kinds of activity but in terms of it actually being an agenda that one might have otherwise adopted as a reason for writing, it's just not enough. Although I can still sense, for example, how the way in which you have openly embraced tradition—although that feels like quite a crass way of describing your relationship to literary history—is something new, it moves things on decisively.

JM: You have to reject your parents but you can accept your grandparents. It's a kind of truism of the way culture works and changes. I remember when Rod Mengham wrote in that *Parataxis* review about my poems in *Imagination Verses* called 'Duets', which are basically cut-ups of Keats and Wordsworth. He read a cheeky irreverence in this gesture, with the assumption was that I had been force-fed these poets, but the fact is nobody offered them to me.[29] So tradition implies that it's been there, and I grew up with this and I want to keep it, which is just a false account of my education and many people's, in this country at least. Tradition might have had a period of stability, from 1930 to 1960, in which it was radical to read Pound. People of the sixties tell that story: "I was only offered this kind of poetry and I had to find Pound". But that situation has been gone for a long time, at least since the seventies. And so for me to go back and find the "tradition" was an act of will.

It's also partly about just being as smart as your predecessors. Pound didn't say, well, I'm not going to read that because it's in the past. Duncan didn't say that, Michael Palmer didn't say that. And for someone to come and say to my generation, well, we read all that and it is worthless so just trust us—no, we have to go back and read for ourselves. Some reject the tradition without having read it or knowing what it is. They're just like, oh that old English poetry. But then you ask, well what exactly do you know about it? If you are going to reject something, it's best to have a reason for doing it.

ST: It kind of imprisons you doesn't it, in a way that you're not even aware of. Because then, like you say, the poets who make that gesture just wind up writing unoriginal poems because they've actually cut themselves off at the root from any way of being discriminating.

JM: I suppose it is similar with religion. My mother rejected Catholicism, and so I was raised that way, but at one point or another I just thought, well, I didn't reject Catholicism, I wasn't oppressed by it, so I don't need to necessarily feel hostile toward it. It's this phrase that one of Steve's mentors, Neil Lazarus, says: you have to know tradition to hate it properly! [**Steve Evans**, in background: It's Adorno!] Oh, it's Adorno, of course it's Adorno! But I love that idea. That's why it might make more sense for me to feel disdain for Beat culture, hippy style. That's my tradition, what I grew up with—guru-ism and smoking pot.

ST: Which is also fraught with its own ambiguities and problems.

---

[29] Mengham wrote: "The technique of cultural appropriation is even more scandalously employed in the poems that advertise their antagonism with the history of English poetry, most obviously the 'duets' with Wordsworth and Keats, which are really duels". See Mengham, 'Reading Jennifer Moxley', 106 (cf. footnote 3).

JM: Right. I grew up with the idea that your politics and your radicality could just be in your lifestyle, and that was an inheritance of the sixties. For me that's something I feel complicated about. We each have our own histories. I feel like some of the critiques of my work that are going down the wrong path are based on this idea that I went to Eton and Oxford, that I'm a boy from fifty years ago! And it's just not my experience! So I feel that the narrative of how literature gets transmitted has not caught up with the reality of what's going on in schools. *The Middle Room* was partly about addressing that issue.

ST: I was going to say it's almost like you're working through your personal version of history in *The Middle Room*, but, in terms of what you've just said, it also seems to be about working through literary history to some extent. Perhaps these are different aspects of the same process. I don't know whether it's quite as simple as placing oneself?

JM: Well, it's like, how do you create a narrative of how you're going to fit into literature? A friend of mine who read it said: "I like the way it shows how you're made and unmade over and over again in your youth". You're constantly about to come together and then you fall apart again and you make big mistakes.

ST: It's not a bad analogue for what happens in a writing career.

JM: Right, exactly.

Caroline Bergvall

This interview was conducted at a café in Manchester on 2 October 2008, and via the internet between Liverpool and London on 14 June 2009.

Scott Thurston: What do you see as the key creative issues facing innovative poets in Britain and North America today?

Caroline Bergvall: I suppose one of the main issues for me might be the wish to think about the role or function of poetry today. What is the role of poetry in a changing world, where reading matters less, where writing is not the immediate inscription used, and where poetry at large is more often than not considered an art of circumstance and occasion? What does this mean for the practice itself? For its readerships? For its diversity and scope?

The demands and forms that cultural, aesthetic, social cohabitation—one's coexistence with others—may have on writing is a key issue. Questions about language-use, translocal experience and cultural flexibility are important too.

And then perhaps closer to the bone: how to be true to one's project, to one's questions, as an artist, as a writer, and not one's allocated cultural slot? The American rap poet Tracie Morris has developed a form of live performance that taps into hip hop and avant-gardist sound poetry. This cuts across many conversations, bridges many chasms, and forces up many questions about identity and oral performance. Charles Bernstein addresses questions of history and knowledge, and manages to give a complex biographic account of Walter Benjamin through the repetitive structures of very simple language games in his poetic opera *Shadowtime*. Alice Oswald in her *Dart* project engages with her process sociologically and ethnographically but then transforms her interviews and conversations into a locative amble along the river. It's about how you manage to locate yourself intellectually and culturally, and how it carries a resonance. I think that's a question that a lot of poets ask themselves.

Then there is the question of innovation as inherited by the avant-gardes. That's a dilemma to do with a particular kind of lineage and how we take that lineage on: whether one accepts it and what one takes from it. Many of the political techniques have become more like formal techniques now. Manovich talks about the PhotoShop effect of avant-garde techniques.[1] Collage found its last political manifestation with the

---

[1] Lev Manovich, *The Language of New Media* (Cambridge, MA: The MIT Press, 1999).

Situationists but since then, and in the cut-and-paste world we live in, does it really have a political frame beyond the self-replication of consumerism? This is exactly why the whole notion of conceptual writing runs the risk of being already outmoded, unless it can become a question to do with engagement, not methodology.[2] The neutralisation of the avant-gardes is completely normal in a way, so where does one look for thinking models? How does one politicise what has become bland and normalised? What kind of methods does one use?

What comes with the question of the avant-garde that is still a crucial one and a difficult one for literature as an institution to cope with is the importance of cross-disciplinarity and cross-culturality. That is what was so powerful in early twentieth century models, like *Parade*, or cubism, or Brecht's music-theatre, or the Negritude project of Senghor and Césaire, or the dream sociology of Mass Observation, and the many forms of cross-genre that came about. I see it in relation to larger tropes such as the rise of technological society, which has informed another kind of urban and telematic living, and implicitly favours interdisciplinary methods. The fact that there was an incremental rise in technologising the bloodbath of wars, and the way European empires finally broke up, yet without letting go of their dangerous neurosis for monologic superiority, is cause for pause. All this is still palpable, unfinished even today. So we might be sitting culturally in distant continuity with the aesthetics of the avant-gardes, but I think there are historical lines, and political awarenesses that cut across all this that still need addressing, in whatever form one chooses.

The stretching of the definition of poetry is one of the issues coming out of literary history that is still full of conflicts and resistance. But I'm also very preoccupied with the outsider status, its degrees. What defines a foreigner, a bicultural resident, a queer citizen, and also and still, the artist? What notions of critical participation does it entail? I think of this much in the sense discussed by Gramsci when he makes a distinction between the expert and the public intellectual. The public intellectual being a necessary and largely willing outsider, a commentating witness, a disturber of the peace.[3] Yet a poet is often seen to be a part of the former,

---

[2] Bergvall notes that the interview took place a few months after her participation in the 'Conceptual Poetry and Its Others' Symposium at the University of Arizona Poetry Center, May 29–31, 2008. Bergvall's paper was entitled 'Social Engagement of Writing' and is viewable at: http://poetrycenter.arizona.edu/conceptualpoetry/cp_media/misc/bergvall.pdf

[3] See Antonio Gramsci's distinction between "organic" and "traditional" intel-

an expert; someone who speaks in a different language about existing conditions. For me, I'm happy that the audience can view or hear or be immersed in something which might have a textual or literary method but they don't necessarily have to take this into account. I like pieces and works that can be quite hard on the reader/viewer/listener, hard in the sense of transforming, tough or crystalline on the body, on the senses and on the mind, and that may have a number of seemingly irreconcilable poetic or artistic methods and histories attached to them. The *Hamletmaschine* (by Heiner Müller) adapted by Einstürzende Neubauten is one example!

On a personal level, a key issue for me that I recognise in many writers, has to do with linguistic use and cultural belonging: what it means and what it does. It is extremely contemporary with our culture today, which flags up a lot of glossic and discursive levels, and where people talk and function side by side, but largely do not communicate with one another. What is happening politically and socially to language and how we speak and how we think in language moves the social right to the heart of writing. It's to do with speaking, with having language, with making language, with meaning and with the rejection of meaning. It is to do with cultural exchange through language, or lack of exchange and how that also reads. What does it mean, beyond language acquisition, that I cannot read the Korean text in Theresa Hak Kyung Cha's *Dictee*[4] and what does this do to the sections of English text that I can read? That's really where this whole idea of innovation in creative practice still matters: it is to do with having an open mind, in one's relation to one's practice's history, as much as to one's current surroundings. Art is about the opening mind.

ST: When I was listening to your performance last night,[5] I actually questioned why I was thinking about your work as *poetry*. Obviously there are all sorts of reasons why, but I began to see the range of processes that you were using as equally recognisable in other contexts of contemporary art practice. I saw this in counterpoint to David Annwn's work which,

---

lectuals' in his piece 'The Intellectuals' in *Selections from the Prison Notebooks* edited by Quintin Hoare and Geoffrey Nowell-Smith (London: Lawrence and Wishart Limited, 1998).
[4] Theresa Hak Kyung Cha, *Dictee* (Berkeley, CA: University of California Press, 2001).
[5] The previous evening Bergvall had performed at the Manchester poetry reading series *The Other Room*, alongside the poet David Annwn and the text-image duo Joy as Tiresome Vandalism. Videos of the performances are archived at: http://otherroom.org/videos/videos_4/.

although also poly-lingual, was rooted in a more bardic style of projection. It's useful for thinking about what innovation means and how one might resist the boxes that are imposed upon one. That said, David has a relationship to Welsh which was less evident in what he was doing last night than your relationship to Norwegian. How were you using Norwegian in the piece from *Plessjør*?

CB: Those were literal translations and work on code-switching. I was trying to create a syntax where both languages actually co-exist and are co-dependent. It is really an exercise in sociolinguistics transformed and used to the full. David's work as I heard it last night was featuring multiple languages, in a way that was grounded in a modernist literary tradition. So the starting point is slightly different. But he referred to Mina Loy, a great example of someone who was troubled by languages, and the gendering of language and art, and the mores of identity, how that shaped her writing. She called herself an "anglo-mongrel". This is a wonderful term that many people today might subscribe to in many different ways, yet with the same sense of bringing something to the table that disturbs the rule and rulers of the English language.

ST: There was also David's poem about Elsa von Freytag-Loringhoven.[6]

CB: The DaDaMaMa. She was fascinating. A powerful and really displaced character.

ST: You read five long pieces each of which had a procedure or a constraint that was quite quickly established, but then one was also immediately aware of a kind of counter-process running through and either breaking down or heightening itself. In *Via*[7] particularly, it starts to create a space in your mind with the layering of the different translations on top of each other so that slight variations suddenly become unusually rich. That's grasping a whole interaction between what I call *method* and *technique*—method as an overall approach and technique as the means you use to execute it—but procedure and process is another distinction that's relevant here

---

[6] See David Annwn's 'Trio Tingel-Tangel Künstlerich' in *Bela Fawr's Cabaret* (West House & Ahadada Books: Sheffield and Urayasu, Japan, 2008), p.103.
[7] 'Via: 48 Dante Variations' in Caroline Bergvall, *Fig: Goan Atom 2* (Great Wilbraham: Salt Publishing, 2005), pp. 6–71. Bergvall describes the project as collating "the opening lines of the *Inferno* translations as archived by the British Library up until May 2000". (p. 64.)

too.[8] I was interested in what you said about the way that certain kinds of techniques which initially had a more politically-charged force in culture are now being reproduced merely as formal exercises. It plays interestingly into issues around teaching innovative practice. For myself, as a lecturer in Creative Writing wanting to pass on a kind of heritage ... that's a dreadful word for it! Tradition is not much better!

CB: What did I say? Lineage? It could be interconnections, both historical and contemporary.

ST: That sounds better! The risk comes when you invite students to reproduce technical procedures, so I try to inform them about the historical significance of these procedures. The hope is to therefore encourage students to find a meaningful relationship to these approaches, so that they are not just reproducing technical strategies without a sense of why those strategies came into being in the first place. Part of the way I try to do this is by putting the rich resources of theoretical writing—that have been part of my training as a student of literature—alongside contemporary writing in order to invite people to make the connection between innovative writing and innovative thinking. I wonder what's your take on that, from your point of view as a teacher but also as a writer? How do you negotiate those relationships between theory and teaching and between theory and practice?

CB: I don't know about your students but very often there is this attitude, especially with those who arrive in Creative Writing of: I don't want to read, I don't want to see work, I'm here to write and get workshopped. It's really bizarre. I think we first have to encourage students to be interested in why they want to be writers and to try to put them at a distance from their own needs. I find that adapting methods of appropriation and transcription, which remove their interiority from the process and highlight the material to hand, very useful. It gives them another kind of conflict than that of their thoughts. It actually starts shifting the way they think about the process. That's one of the first things I think about, rather than literary theory. It's really: let me put you and your interior need at a distance first, and then let's see what happens. Then we can start having some fun with

---

[8] See Scott Thurston, 'Allen Fisher—Reading "Mummers' Strut"' in Volume 4 of *Eseje o współczesnej poezji brytyjskiej i irlandzkiej*, (*Essays on Modern British and Irish Poetry*) ed. by Ludmiła Gruszewska and David Malcolm, (Gdańsk: University of Gdańsk Press, 2005), pp. 119–134.

the methods in front of us. From there I have a tendency to move towards examples taken from a mix of poetic works, visual arts or sound arts that use language. They're so literate when it comes to audio-visual work and the visual arts world, and yet can also be profoundly and strangely unliterary. I have a tendency to bring all that in quite quickly, to show what kind of processes there might be in these artists' use of language that could be of interest to us as writers. After that the field of literature and poetry opens up quite naturally through curiosity and detail work. You might say it's a backwards way of doing things and I wouldn't stick to this every time. To an extent it does stem from teaching practice in arts colleges, where the model is not necessarily literary. And for the rest it is my resolutely cross-disciplinary bias. We want to train writers that are critically-engaged so that hopefully when they leave they want to use their skills and their thoughts to take part in their culture, our culture. That's the ideal isn't it? Those questions are part of the basis of the pedagogy in a way: why is writing important, or is it? Is innovation in art important and what kind of innovation are we talking about?

ST: I often ask myself that: am I doing something very niche or clearing a space for things to happen? Contemporary practice has such a history to draw on and there are so many models. They may not be ones that students will be able to relate to immediately, but they just need to work at it a bit to start to build up their own sets of references. I've been re-reading Deleuze recently and thinking about his view that philosophy creates new concepts. It feels like an inherently creative approach, and that's why I'm trying to introduce his work to my students at the moment.

CB: I think Deleuze and Guattari's view of literature and language in their book on Kafka, and their concept of a minor literature that is not identity-based but more about development in language, is very useful.[9] Also, of course the French crew, Kristeva, Barthes, Derrida, Genette, bring out a lot of important issues to do with semiotics, the historicity of writing and politics within textual genres. A linguist such as Jakobson and the Prague Circle is crucial as a tie-in between language, communication and literary practice. For contemporary issues inspired by this, Stuart Hall, Paul Gilroy and Gayatri Spivak but also Judith Butler provide the ground

---

[9] See 'What is a Minor Literature?' in Gilles Deleuze and Félix Guattari, *Kafka: Towards a Minor Literature* trans. by Dana Polan (Minneapolis: University of Minnesota Press, 1986), pp. 16–27.

for discussions around identitarian constraints and what that does to one's writing. It's not Lit Theory *per se* but more often than not it has language at its core. I'm looking at audio texts at the moment with some students, and we've just been discussing Ginsberg's use of tape recording for writing. I've paired this with a small section from Alvin Lucier's *I am sitting in a room* and a chapter from Friedrich Kittler's *Gramophone, Film, Typewriter*.

ST: In terms of the history of your own writing, how much has literary and cultural theory had an impact?

CB: Judith Butler and Foucault were really important to me, as were the thinkers I just mentioned! Their examination of identity and of the frameworks in which power sits, not only in and through language but also in the wider social context, were crucial to me. One of the starting points is to investigate identity, its framework, its prison, as well as its potentially liberatory aspects. If you're gay, the liberatory aspect of identity is not so clear, on the contrary, it can seem more like an imposed framework. All of that was very important to my writing: this notion that nothing is a given and yet all might be taken for granted and for reasons that have nothing to do with me. This has been really crucial to the development of my personal thinking in relation to my work.

In the early nineties I was particularly engaged in thinking about the concept of the hybrid,[10] and the notion of multiculturalism. The questions that emerged concern the neo-imperialism of the term, the homogeneity of that kind of plurality, the way it starbucks the whole of coffee, the way it pretends to mixity, while languages, genders, participants get erased that do not fit. This connects with work on my ongoing piece *Cropper*, in which you have this whole abstracted notion of bodies, or languages, as entities that get pushed aside, or get categorised, or get evacuated or shut out. It's to do both with socially minoritarian identities and linguistically foreigning identities. There's a fundamental displacement but the question at home, close to the bone, what is difference, does not get addressed.

I really believe in a personal starting point, that if you put your experience at the heart of your own question as a writer or as an artist, it's about how you answer that question of who you are and why you are like this and why you speak like this. I read critically to try and get to the heart of my own dilemmas, and the things that prevent or forward my possible

---

[10] Key theorists would include Gayatri Chakravorty Spivak and Homi Bhaba.

participation in the world.

To return to teaching, once you feel that students are starting to be confidently playful, that they're really starting to enjoy playing, then you can start them thinking about their own cultural belonging and what they think of their gender. This is not so that we can get to "confessional" stuff, but so that we can get to critical stuff about the way we are constructed gender-wise and socially and what it's doing to us. I think that's very important. That's one way I think critical thinking ties-in: it's there because you are provoked by things in the world that are about you and that you seek out.

Another way in which theory ties-in is more to do with learning your trade and being interested in the methods of your trade, which could be literature or poetics or visual arts and so on. I think it's crucial that we have as big a pool of knowledge as possible, so that we know where we come from trade-wise, even if we don't necessarily use it. I really enjoy reading critical texts written by writers or artists, because they have so much to teach me as a writer. I've read a lot of Heiner Müller, the East German playwright, for example. I read Cixous more for her critical work than her fiction. She was brought up in Algeria, as was Derrida. Derrida wrote a wonderful book on monolingualism, about not having a mother tongue.[11] These are citizens brought up in occupied territory, where your language, your family's language, your culture's language—or is it your body's language?—is disallowed. Derrida's very interesting on what that creates and Cixous also pursues it in *Rootprints*.[12]

ST: It's heartening to hear you talk in such a way when some would have us think that such work is irrelevant now.

CB: We're in a culture where politically we're encouraged to be non-intellectuals and by and large, non-critical. We're being asked to swallow what's happening, and to stick very close to each our own separate condition. We're asked not to show broader empathy or engagement, nor to engage with what happens to others; not to be too polemical, unless we are directly connected. It's so dangerous. We're all connected. In my piece 'More Pets' I set up a very simple structure that is ruled by a domestic

---

[11] Jacques Derrida, *Monolingualism of the Other or, The Prosthesis of Origin* trans. by Patrick Mensah (Palo Alto, CA: Stanford University Press, 1998).
[12] Hélène Cixous and Mireille Calle-Gruber, *Rootprints: Memory and Life Writing* trans. by Eric Prenowitz (London: Routledge, 1997).

bestiary, comparatives and visual dashes: "a more—cat", "a more—dog" etc and then it develops into these weird interrelated morphic bodies.[13] Lots of people come up to me with great comments for that piece.

ST: I'm going to work with it with my students next week, among other texts in *Fig*.

CB: It's just a very simple means to tap into a more profound statement!

ST: But the implications of it are considerable. It's nice to hear that it already has a reputation in terms of its reception. What's the method in the Chaucer pieces? Are you actually writing through the tales themselves?

CB: No, but I'm reading *The Canterbury Tales* all the time at the moment, and reading a lot around Middle English and Middle French, and Scandinavian sagas. I'm finding myself in this big cultural moment in the history of the English language, and Chaucer's become a pretext to look at the language in the making, the literature in the making. My version of 'The Host's Tale' is an appropriative exercise, it's composed of food and drink references in *The Canterbury Tales* that I read in Middle English. I've got another one which is 'The Not Tale (funeral)' which is actually twenty lines of the funeral of Arcite in 'The Knight's Tale'. I took those lines, which I find very beautiful, and just basically condensed them, removing the meat of the funerary descriptions, leaving just the bone.[14] 'The Summer Tale' is based on a BBC article I found about the Pope's visit to Poland, which I used to polemicise rather gently against current religious hypocrisy. 'Alyson Singes' has been based so far on the Wife of Bath's massive prologue which is so extraordinary. I've enjoyed thinking about what kind of a statement a woman like that would make today, what kind of a woman that might be. All of these texts also deal with what kind of English I need to write in. So there's some Middle English but also contemporary English, like the section that uses pop music references. It becomes a pretext to look at contemporary English. My Alyson is still tied to the Wife of Bath's prologue, but it's now developing into a larger framework involving Emma Goldman and Vivienne Westwood among others. What's wonderful about

---

[13] See 'More Pets' in Bergvall, *Fig* (2005), pp. 83–89. An example of one of the weird bodies might be "a rabbitnot–catnot chatchat" (p. 89).
[14] See 'The Knight's Tale', lines 2913–2966. Bergvall's treatment owes something to the narrator's conceit in these lines about what he will *not* tell the reader: "I wol nat tellen" (l. 2963), whilst simultaneously describing the funeral.

a project like this is that I'm also finding myself at the start of the literary, at the brink between manuscript and print culture, a manuscript culture where the written text is largely spoken but also passed and read, so it's all in the mix.[15]

ST: When I first heard that you were working with Chaucer I was surprised because it seemed such a literary reference compared to your usual sources.

CB: Yes, to an extent. It won't necessarily stay like that, but I only envisage it as an audio-file—it was published first on-line as an audio-file[16]—and as a book at the end of the project. I haven't developed a book like this before. *Fig* and *Goan Atom* were projects that had had another life, and that I assembled into book form. I never thought about the amount of time it takes to actually genuinely write a book before because I tend to work on projects of varying lengths from three months to a year. It's a very different sense of time—temporality is showing up in the method. I need time in a very different way than when I'm involved in some of my more audio-visual projects or collaborations.

ST: I'm having the opposite experience writing a poem for a performance in a park in Liverpool. I've been settled into a regular writing practice for the last three or four years which has produced two lengthy sequences in which time plays a role almost as a compositional device. Now, however, I'm suddenly thrown out of that regular practice in all sorts of unpredictable ways by having to work to a deadline. But I'm finding that it's very good for me to be forced to work in a different way.

CB: To rethink your relation to time?

ST: Yes.

[*End of Manchester interview*]

---

[15] For an overview see Caroline Bergvall, 'Short Aside to "The Franker Tale"', *Jacket* 32 (April 2007). Viewable at http://jacketmagazine.com/32/p-bergvall-franker-aside.shtml
[16] See Penn Sound: http://writing.upenn.edu/pennsound/x/Bergvall.php

ST: I wanted to ask you about your concept of tactical authorship.[17] It appealed to me because one of the main reasons I'm drawn to investigating your work is the diversity of practices that you work across, whether it's writing for the page or video or gallery installation. I wondered if tactical authorship linked up to that approach?

CB: The starting point for me is De Certeau's notion of the difference between strategy and tactics at the beginning of *The Practice of Everyday Life*. He argues that the tactical is what is not institutionalised or does not have a full, proper place in which to function. He writes that: "the place of a tactic belongs to the other, a calculus which cannot count on a proper, spatial institution or localisation nor on a borderline distinguishing the other as a visible totality".[18] He then moves on to talking about everyday practices that are tactical in character. I was interested in that because of the connection between art practice, language and everyday life actions; the everyday as a vast field of both fossilisation and potential. There is also the Duchampian idea of the *infra-thin* as the immeasurability of the impact of micro-events, occurrences. He mentions the heat felt when sitting down in a bus seat just vacated by another passenger.[19] Georges Perec had a similar notion of the *infraordinary*, developed in many ways on the back of his disillusion with the May '68 revolution, its bombast and failure, as a way to reconnect with the micro-events of history inscribed within daily actions, daily objects, ways of bringing the unobserved into one's observation field.[20]

Strictly speaking the term is primarily used in relation to the guerrilla principles of "tactical media" that are interventionist ways by which

---

[17] See Caroline Bergvall, 'Pressure Points: Gendered and Tactical Authorship' *How2* (2008). Viewable at: http://www.asu.edu/pipercwcenter/how2journal/vol_3_no_3/bergvall/bergvall-pressure-points.html
[18] Michel de Certeau, *The Practice of Everyday Life* (Berkeley, CA and London: University of California Press, 1984), p. 9.
[19] "Fire without smoke, the warmth of a seat which has just been left, reflection from a mirror or glass, watered silk, iridescent, the people who go through [subway gates] at the very last moment, velvet trousers, their whistling sound, is an infra-thin separation signalled". Marcel Duchamp, *Notes*, arranged and translated by Paul Matisse (Boston: G. K. Hall, 1983), p. 45.
[20] "What's really going on, what we're experiencing, the rest, all the rest, where is it? How should we take account of, question, describe what happens every day and recurs every day: the banal, the quotidian, the obvious, the common, the ordinary, the infra-ordinary, the background noise, the habitual?" Georges Perec, 'Approaches to *What?*' from 'L'Infra-ordinaire' (1989) in *Species of Spaces and Other Pieces* (London: Penguin, 2008), p. 209–10.

thinkers, artists, activists enter, or dis-enter, or dissenter the public spheres; turning media workings against themselves to circulate other messages. These interventions are led by attention-raising events-led interventions. They're performative and activist. They cut through the inertia and hold of broadcasting and the fat of institutional discourses. The Iranian twitter revolution we're just experiencing must be one of its more surprising, radical and empowering examples. The group of lesbians abseiling into the House of Commons at the time of Clause 28 during the live broadcast news ensured the debate was kept in public view and has become an iconic moment. The filmed infiltrations of the Yes Men into a World Health Organisation meeting also play into this.

Many artists see their art's resonance in similar tactical ways. It is the only way to respond. To tackle the system, its tentacular hold, not only with sudden displays, but also with intense lines of connectivity. It's not a systemic attitude. But it has stopped suffering from the impossibility of explicit political engagement and is discovering a differently participatory mode of resisting, of raising attention, of handling the surrounding events. It is not nervous about simplifications, it uses them back. I see Juliana Spahr's *This Connection of Everyone With Lungs* (2005) around the Iraq war and media overflow very much in that light, or Krzysztof Wodiczko's guerrilla projection of the Nazi flag on South Africa House (1985). The latter seemed in many ways an old-fashioned avant-gardist showdown. It was powerful exactly because it disobeyed the idea that art can no longer act in this way. It turned it on its head, while keeping the button pushed on apartheid at the same time.

Anyway, I actually used the term in a talk I was asked to develop around *l'écriture féminine* and forms of feminism at a writers' conference.[21] As a socio-political phenomenon, feminism in the West is being pushed underground. One is told one cannot act or write on the strength of the term alone. Yet the term has long since broken up into many specific factions of interest and of struggle. Issues tied to questions of gender and power are as deep as ever. The terms set by ongoing feminist revolutions about the world are still radical. I was a teen during the Greenham Common peace camp. I witnessed the feminist marches of the 70s only on the TV. In a sense I'm deeply connected to this shift between large scale

---

[21] See footnote 17. The talk was presented at 'Feminaissance'—a colloquium on women, experimental writing and feminism, 27-28 April 2007, at the Museum of Contemporary Art, Los Angeles.

collective resistance and more individual or dispersed tactical means. How does a writer who feels herself/himself to carry feminist awareness displace, rethink the modes through which it will continue to shake things up. It can be through symbolic tropes. Questions of liminality, of in-betweenness, of borders, of false perspectives, or questions of fluency or non-fluency, of the hybrid, all these are rich and complex fields that dictate body and language constructedness, spatial occupancy, social myth. Each can be applied to actual social mores, the playing fields of power and justice, to the making of imagination and of revolt.

ST: Would you say therefore that the formal diversity of your practice is a conscious attempt to work against more conservative notions of consistency?

CB: Well, it's more to do with finding the law of the work in the methods and materials of the work. There's an internal logic to a piece that takes it to a certain place. It's a connection between the means and the idea. An aspect of its context or the methods it uses also directs the idea of the piece. In a way, consistency becomes a non-issue because I am applying my work to projects, to methods, to contexts. I feel that the consistency of the work might appear over time, across pieces, and environments, rather than for me to make an effort at a formal consistency, one that might be based on literary modes or following a homogeneous trajectory as a writer. I used to really love Flaubert's work and that certainly is an oeuvre that does not appear consistent. He tries out a different way of writing according to the project he's tackling. In a sense, that's his consistency, that dedication to a particular kind of research and rigour. I do think that there's a consistency of approach in always remaining open to the methods or the ideas that might present themselves or that one wishes to pursue. I'm reminded of Bakhtin's notion that closure is in the structural logic of the work, not its plot or narrative.[22] Perhaps there's a consistency of thinking, of exploring, of moving from project to project, yielding similar tropes or *leitmotifs*, putting them to the test of another ground, another sentence: the existential trajectory of making work.

ST: So it's more something that emerges as an inherent integrity rather than something which is intentionally driven?

---

[22] See M. M. Bakhtin, *The Dialogic Imagination: Four Essays* (Austin: University of Texas Press, 1982).

CB: In a sense. But this is a complex issue for me. It's a dilemma between how the complexities of art engage—currently a taboo word—a historic notion at one extreme, and formal and some conceptual practices at the other, with critical aesthetics in the middle as a sort of holding station of commitment and material practice. It internalises political dilemma, the protest voice, yet it doesn't know how to use it and yet doesn't want to let go of it. Bob Ostertag is a great example of this. He's a composer working a lot with the sampling of social situations. In his piece *All the Rage* (1993) he covers a gay liberation march in San Francisco at the height of the AIDS crisis. Increasingly the voices become filtered by his frequency treatments so that what starts to emerge is a drone of protest, rather than the protest itself, a feeling of rage, rather than that rage, while the tone of the phrases, the lines, get picked up by instruments. So it becomes quite abstracted. It's a weird feeling. It's as though he wishes to render the collective impulse and also profoundly individualise his response to it. Jacques Rancière's ideas about this are exciting: that some art modalities might currently be asked to carry embryonic political impulses, because the notion of collectivity has disbanded, has been disbanded. The barricades are no longer where we think they are. A barricade today might be a floating plank in the flooding, or a specific accent kept in the mouth.[23]

My starting points are often caught in this dilemma, in this questioning about the writer's responsibility and the liberatory reality of art itself. It is only as I work that I come to greater clarity, in a sense that I dare to think more fully, that I can let my anger or my passion fuel the work until it drops away, takes its place in the work, and that other elements can guide me. By then the structure's in place, the materials are working, the research is done, so it all makes sense that I can change gear, accelerate, increase the motivation of the work, its thought processes, without being too directive. It's all to do with architectonics, and collaborative premises, but I still wish at times I knew how to write down the short, sharp, hard-hitting pieces I sometimes wake up with!

ST: In your research notes on *How 2* for 'About Face' you note the intent to: "denaturalise social identities and politicize a heterogeneity of means while not sacrificing neither critical experimentalism nor the crucial politics of

---

[23] "Suitable political art would ensure, at one and the same time, the production of a double effect: the readability of a political signification and a sensible or perceptual shock caused, conversely, by the uncanny, by that which resists signification". Jacques Rancière, *The Politics of Aesthetics* (London: Continuum, 2008), p. 63.

participation."[24] How might the diversity of method actually risk losing critical experimentalism or participation?

CB: One risk is that cross-art practices, or practices that use a number of tools and histories, fall between chairs or between cultures. Commercial publishing is a very conservative environment—primarily because it's caught up in a type of book culture which it holds on to very aggressively—and it means that anything that doesn't fit within this book definition is actually not viable. But really what matters is to work where and how one feels one resonates best, and where one's ideas connect the most. I may no longer be as literary as I was, but literature is my starting-point, my first knowledge base, and when I apply what it teaches me in projects that go beyond the page it is because the question I ask about language perhaps comes together in a way that excites me beyond my comfort zone, sometimes beyond explicit writing, or in the confluence of writing with sounding and with spatialising.

There's no resistance in me towards literature as an artform, as a mode of manifesting and thinking in language and with languages. On the contrary. It just seems to me that following on from the great technological revolutions of the twentieth century and now its digital continuation, it needs to accommodate more modes of writing. When I think about the future of the book, what interests me is the social issue about the dissemination of written language and what this can do to one's use of language. As Johanna Drucker[25] sees it, and many with her, following on from the illustrated books of the nineteenth century and even early illuminated manuscripts, and through the print performances of Dada and Surrealism and Concrete, the book may soon become a very specific environment where it is used nearly as a sculptural object, or as an installed object, and artists use the pages as a sort of event. We're talking in very different cultural terms in this case. To consider the future of the *literary* book: the novel, for instance, is a print-bound form which came about very much through the dissemination of written culture. Yet through the audiobook culture it has proven to be immensely amenable to being sold as recordings. I remember David Antin talking about these issues of

---

[24] See Caroline Bergvall, 'Piece in Progress: About Face (*Goan Atom*, 2)', *How2* (2001). Viewable at: http://www.asu.edu/pipercwcenter/how2journal/archive/online_archive/v1_6_2001/current/in-conference/bergvall.html
[25] See, for example, Johanna Drucker, *The Century of Artists' Books*, (New York: Granary Books, 1995).

orality and literature in his book with Charles Bernstein.[26] There was the surprising sense that although Antin does all these talk pieces, that for him the final achievement for his work is that it finds its place in book form. I found that very ironic but also a sign of the book still being a writer's mark of recognition. Poetry of course can quite easily inhabit any world, old or new, printed or heard, sculpted or installed. It depends on its cultural marker, its semiotic encoding, at any given time. It is archaic yes, and it is a million-headed form.

ST: Staying with these issues of the book environment, and going back to the first part of *Goan Atom*, it struck me when re-reading it that one way to approach it is as a series of actions in space, rather than as unfolding a particular argument. It might be a false opposition, because it isn't only a series of acts in space; there's language there and terms and concepts which have a particular meaning.

CB: I like the phrase "series of actions"! It's accurate because some of these pieces had also been installations or had come out of performances. *Ambient Fish*, for example, was part of an installation and I had written 'Doll' and 'jets-poupee' from the context of a series of Hans Bellmer photographs. It's inaccurate, however, because primarily I consider the piece to be an abstract play. I have always enjoyed reading plays. And during the period of *Goan Atom* I was reading Aristophanes, on recommendation from Stacy Doris, as well as Alfred Jarry's *Ubu Roi* (1896). I was also looking at Aeschylus and the fact that there are, perhaps obviously, no written stage directions. Everybody's a voice or nothing: a sign, a mark, or nothing. It makes an entrance, it speaks. If robbed of speech, it is robbed of life. It's a play of voices; a choral piece, and of course the chorus is fundamental in Aeschylus. The backdrop is the page. If you start looking at *Goan Atom* as a sort of play, it makes another kind of sense. The visual interventions into reading and the spatial set-up could be about staging an encounter of characters, a scene played out. The relation to the reader is also to engage with a performative or spatialised approach to reading. You have the play playing on the reader: turning the pages, having to negotiate the white space, the little "s"s, turning the pages around. There are a lot of small visual episodes that take place—the Gertrude Stein episode, the Cindy Sherman

---

[26] David Antin and Charles Bernstein, *A Conversation with David Antin* (New York: Granary Books, 2002). Reviewed by Caroline Bergvall in *Jacket* 22 (May 2003). Viewable at: http://jacketmagazine.com/22/bergv-antin.html

episode, the Louise Bourgeois episode—that are based on drawings or photos or text sections. Their voices come in to refer to these events and to connect them up to this generalised world of the doll. It doesn't have a unity of time-space-action, but it is in three acts, even if ironically, and it does have some of the markers that indicate that this is speech and action, and therefore reading it is also an address to the reader or the potential performer/s.

ST: The notion of it as a play is really useful.

CB: I suppose it forms the mould into which I put that material in the final instance. It also shows my interest in how plays as a literary form reproduce speech, or rather, stage it. There's a process of staging on the pages of this book—through the naming and the boldfaces—that points towards a tradition of representing plays and performances for the page. It reminds me of the unperformable directions of many Jackson Mac Low pieces. Not unperformable at all in fact, but excruciating directives to read and engage with. But then we deal here also with a tradition of sound notation. The German writer Elfriede Jelinek in her play *Der Tod und das Mädchen I–V* (2003) insults the potential stage director before they even get started. "Just don't think you can do it this way or that way…" and then proceeds to tell them they can light it however they choose. The stage directions become these wonderful moments of regret, intense forms of reluctance in relinquishing the control of written speech, of its future manifestation. Fluxus tapped into that in a way, being one long series of exercises in extraordinary and extraordinarily banal stage directions, for the use of any performer-person; instructional pieces, as they were called.[27]

ST: To change tack, I was interested in following through our earlier discussion on the importance of multilingualism for your work and your

---

[27] "The first examples of what were to become Fluxus event scores date back to John Cage's famous class at The New School, where artists such as George Brecht, Al Hansen, Allan Kaprow, and Alison Knowles began to create art works and performances in musical form. One of these forms was the event. Events tend to be scored in brief verbal notations. These notes are known as event scores. In a general sense, they are proposals, propositions, and instructions. Thus, they are sometimes known as proposal pieces, propositions or instructions." From the introduction to *The Fluxus Performance Workbook* ed. by Ken Friedman, Owen Smith and Lauren Sawchyn (Performance Research e-Publications, 2002). Viewable at: http://www.thing.net/~grist/ld/fluxus-workbook.pdf

personal experience of it.

CB: *Cropper* explores this whole idea of using or developing a form of writing as an account of my personal experience of multilingualism. For the second edition, I rethought the piece because I wanted to make it much more explicitly committed to an autobiographical take on multilingualism. I was thinking again about what multilingualism actually means, and how one addresses linguistic and textual material with autobiographical content. The piece now divides into two sections: the first is the "autobiographic sketch" and the second is a much more performative, almost anthemic text, in which the personal testimony opens into a more collective experience of the difficulties of accounting for others and for oneself.

It's been published twice, once in 2006 and now in 2008, and I think the changes to the first part are primarily to do with the fact that I started engaging much more explicitly with methods of spelling, and also that I now give an account of the different language trajectories that I've made personally. It recounts in a very stylised way how and why I went from this language through to this language and the different questions that were posed on these journeys. It really deals with the consequences of the subjective experience of multilingualism on the writer. It asks what the textual dimension is of that experience.

I've written quite a lot about this theme in different pieces—the whole idea of how writers tackle language belonging or cultural belonging. Explicitly bilingual writers that have made an impression on me include Theresa Cha, Lisa Linn Kanae and Coco Fusco in their polemics of using work as a linguistic obstacle course. It seems to me that the fact of belonging is the main issue of bilingualism or biculturalism. There's an immense inventive flexibility that derives from bilingualism. But this can also be a way of tackling often pressing concerns tied to biculturalism when it clashes with discourses around nationalism, citizenship, loyalty as a monolingual value, prejudice around one of one's identities. All of this becomes immediately part of the questions asked in big and small ways, when you are a bilingual writer, if you place that as part of the project of writing. 'A Cat in the Throat' is a short piece on *Jacket*[28] which starts out of exactly that notion, through Spivak, of what the "here" is, where you are, what does it mean, and how you handle this notion of

---

[28] See Caroline Bergvall, 'A Cat in the Throat: On Bilingual Occupants' *Jacket* 37 (January 2009). Viewable at: http://jacketmagazine.com/37/bergvall-cat-throat.shtml

multilingualism. Spivak is Asian-American, and in India multilingualism is the norm. You have some leading languages, but the norm is that languages criss-cross and have their own bounded logic. Spivak also points to other issues to do with literacy as well as the diglossic aspect of power in the multilingualism of India. This is very different from the UK where we are in a monolingual culture with an enormous number of communities that each speak languages that are kept back from a general national make-up, and yet artistically we can see the influence on British culture of bicultural citizens. This is very much connected to my AHRC fellowship, which is called 'Writing in Tongues'.

ST: Can we pursue this notion of the "autobiographic sketch"?

CB: Philippe Lejeune describes autobiography as a chronology of events that is narrated from the beginning to a perceived end.[29] This is such a crude view of narrative temporality, of the chaos of memory, of the loss of control of language. I think about autobiographic literature, especially late twentieth-century literature—and also critical literature which deals with autobiography—as, on the contrary, trying to give an account of subjectivity. Therefore it's less about a chronology of your personal life and more about tracing the questions that are connected to subjectivity, to the making of the subject, and, to the making of the writer and the writing. I find these kinds of questions very interesting because you move away from a confessional or chronological approach, but retain that involvement of the person's existential field in the methods used in the development of the writing. I'm interested in the way W.G. Sebald, for example, deals with autobiography as a form of research and fictionalisation that allows him to bring in lost histories and to make connections between, say, a labyrinth, Manchester and his visit to the translator Michael Hamburger.[30] This approach allows him to set up realms of associations between experiences— or between things collated—and the project of the writing.

I suppose my first interest in this theme came through reading the *nouveau roman* writer Nathalie Sarraute's book *Enfance* (1983) [tr. *Childhood*] in which she questions the autobiographic enterprise and tries to tackle it by trying to remember some Russian words. She comes from

---

[29] In Lejeune conceptualises autobiography as a "retrospective prose narrative that a real person creates about his own existence when he emphasizes individual life, particularly the history of his personality". Philippe Lejeune, *Autobiographical Pact* (Paris: Seuil, 1974), p. 14.
[30] See W.G. Sebald, *The Emigrants* (London: Vintage, 2002).

a family of Russian emigrants. She tries to pronounce the words but they don't mean what she thinks they mean, and in fact in the end she simply can't remember what they mean. I'm interested in these tropic lines that organise the subjective account rather than the chronology of living. My favourite autobiographic work is a very short piece: Georges Perec's 'The Rue Vilin' about the gradual destruction accounted for in the text, of his childhood street.[31] And then of course Christian Boltanski's childhood photos, where he uses similar postures of boys he found, and tags them as himself growing up.[32] Believing a portrait is just about the way it can posture. Like those endless photos of bespectacled writers pictured at their desk.

ST: Is your autobiographic writing likely to develop? It's there in parts of the Chaucer piece and *Plessjør*.

CB: Yes. Indirectly it's also there in the notes of *Goan Atom 2*, with all the process and method material about where I've shown this piece and so on. That material is part of the autobiographical, autographical account of the existence of a piece but therefore also where I am in the thinking of the piece. I came across John Tranter's notes on his book *Urban Myths* (2006), and they struck me as an extraordinary example of an audiovisual, critical autobiography made by a poet, using his work as the starting point. They're wonderful—full of erudition and ludism, and illustrated with black and white personal photos of his trips to the Middle East and reproductions of poems.[33] It's extremely rich and has that labyrinthine quality that we get with associative memory.

ST: This is a thread that has become stronger as I've been conducting this project—it's there in everybody's work but in very different ways. Karen talks about *Implexures* as a "poly-biography", then there's Jennifer's autobiography tracing her development as a poet. It's something that was less obvious to me in your work when I first approached it, but now it's coming through very clearly.

CB: Perhaps we're all getting older! Stendhal's *The Life of Henri Brulard* (1835–36, pub. 1890), a book I've always loved, starts "I'm going to be fifty".

---

[31] See Perec, *Species of Spaces*, pp. 212–221.
[32] See Christian Boltanski, *10 photographic portraits of Christian Boltanski 1946–1964* (1972).
[33] Viewable at http://johntranter.com/notes/um.shtml

That's what propels him to write this extraordinary wandering, meandering book with its tiny ink sketches of maps and locations as though one might one day get there oneself, to those streets, to those houses. In *Three Steps on the Ladder of Writing* (1994), Cixous has written some great pages on this book: the fact that he needs to rip at his undergarment to quickly write down the list of his past loves sets up a beautiful and fanciful meditation about writing and desire.

ST: Given the autobiographical and bilingual elements in *Plessjør*, can you explain how the title works? It reads like a cross-linguistic pun on "pleasure".

CB: That's right. I had to write to a number of Norwegian friends asking them how to spell "pleasure" in Norwegian, and they all agreed that this would work. Of course it doesn't! Initially I had put a "k" instead of the second "s" to give "skj", because that's "sh" in Norwegian, but I changed it to that "o" with a bar across, which means "uh" or "er". Anyway, it is more or less recognisable as "pleasure" although in fact no-one can pronounce it or understand it, so it's an inkblot with a bar across.

ST: What I found interesting about this book is the way in which it is aware of textuality even when you are not using language. In '21 Love Poems', for example, the ruled lines on the page look like a template for a poem. Even the toeprints are placed in what looks like a kind of text-bearing structure.

CB: That's right—they're organised and gridded-up.

ST: I was fascinated by how you take writing to the edge almost of body art here.

CB: It has something to do with body art, to mud and paint performances of the seventies with those clear body gestures of the toes and the nipple. In that sense it is quite illustrative in its relation to pleasure and performance and it means to be. And '21 Love Poems' is written for love and as a love piece. At every end of these ink lines there's a sliding of the ink. This was both intensely pleasurable and unnerving, like being unable to brush off a fear about something, love's temporariness and certainty, a jolting memory. Making something beautiful when all feels beautiful brings it all up. It was drawn while re-reading Adrienne Rich's sequence of the same title.[34] But

---

[34] Adrienne Rich, *Twenty-one Love Poems* (Emeryville, CA: Effie's Press, 1976).

there was quite another process behind this book too. I had an invitation to write a book for a Norwegian publisher, but found myself again unable to write in Norwegian! So there's a sense of the difficulty of entering that language as a writer and of looking for alternative ways of thinking about writing, so that it could be accessible "as" Norwegian. I ended up with something that has more to do with mark-making: going all the way back to the basics of writing. There's a connection here with Henri Michaux, who produced what Artaud called "written drawings", or with Cy Twombly on the act of mark-making as a process of language acquisition, because we learn by tracing these letters along long lines.[35]

Although I'm fully literate and fluent in Norwegian, the question was: if I'm going to remove myself from the process of writing in that language, what can I propose in return? What I proposed was really the entry to writing: the process of making lines that will lead to language. The four words that form the piece "much møkk ånd hand" mean something in both Norwegian and English, so you have a synthesising of that process with a very stylized, visual way of presenting the writing. The idea of finding an alternative therefore becomes quite internationalist. I recently came across Steiner again, arguing that literature is one of the arts that has been very strong in English culture but doesn't cross frontiers easily. I couldn't just resort to translating from another language because the project was about being in that specific language and at that specific border. So I devised the process that I've been describing in order to provide a project that was, as you rightly say, textually-informed. When the project was finished I wrote that final piece in which I then just went to English and was able to feed in some lines in Norwegian. It's a writer's project and yet it openly uses another kind of literacy to cope with the impossibility for me of crossing into a specific language in writing. Paradoxically, the text it ended up producing—and the same applies perhaps to the final section of *Cropper*—is a very focused, tight and powerful piece in English, with Norwegian as a prompt and a sidekick. Both texts carry a strong sense of commitment, and they dare to reach for love in a way I rarely do in my work, and do so in a depersonalised way. This has been a really powerful kick for me.

[35] See Caroline Bergvall, 'Handwriting as a Form of Protest: Fiona Templeton's *Cells of Release*', *Jacket* 26 (October 2004). Viewable at: http://jacketmagazine.com/26/berg-temp.html and Caroline Bergvall, 'Body & Sign: Some thoughts around the work of Aaron Williamson, Hannah Weiner, and Henri Michaux', *Jacket* 22 (May 2003). Viewable at: http://jacketmagazine.com/22/berg-body.html

Talking Poetics

ST: Why do you think it was impossible for you to approach it in Norwegian?

CB: I don't know. I've lived in Norway—I was a journalist even—but when it comes to poetics I've just never been able to find a way of approaching language that felt adequate to me in Norwegian, until now. Perhaps it's a bit of a cliché to say it like this, but in a sense I have found my third term—my own term—in the third language of English. Now, of course, I've been functioning in English so much that I've been establishing myself as a writer in English. Beckett had this ability to go into French and translate himself back, but this is not something I've been able to do.

When I'd written 'The Host's Tale', I argued to a Norwegian magazine that this could have been close to Norwegian because when Scandinavian audiences hear me read it they find it very funny because of how it sounds! Although I perform it with a Scandinavian slant, the magazine was happy to publish it in the Middle English. I think I take all my freedom and my enjoyment of language as a starting point in English and then I move it over. But if I'm asked to move over completely, for some reason that doesn't work for me.

ST: I think that was what I was trying to get at earlier with that question about the subjective experience of multilingualism. What you're saying reveals that you have different relationships to different languages. Perhaps it is because you've found a particular relationship to English that a lot of your creative thinking has gone into your work in that language and that's where your thinking is focused. It's interesting to think about it as a process—being in various linguistic environments and then finding yourself in one where new possibilities emerge.

CB: Absolutely. I consider *Plessjør* to be a bilingual piece. The book asks what kind of iconic structures or objects a speaker, an actant sets up to be recognisable and/or to recognise her surroundings—lines, grids, ink marks and so on. It's a direct consequence of the investment in bilingual issues that we've been describing: how one resorts sometimes not just to non-verbal body art but also to its other extremity, the multitudes of articulate languages.

ST: It's a fascinating response to that situation.

Andrea Brady

This interview was conducted at Andrea Brady's house in North London on 27 May 2009.

Scott Thurston: To start with something really concrete, I'd like to ask about how the poems come into being: do they have particular occasions, techniques? What's your process of composition?

Andrea Brady: I think the practice divides into two categories. On the one hand there are poems of occasion, poems which emerge out of what Pater would describe as periods of intense susceptibility, where you feel that you are a kind of sounding board to language in the environment and within your own personal dialogues and in the news and so forth. That all accrues to a critical mass, and if that coincides helpfully with a poetic mood and an opportunity to write then it can result in the production of what I would refer to as an occasional poem. Those are the poems which for me tend to be most intensely lyrical or, if not inward-looking, at least inward-reflecting. Even though they consist of material which is gathered from the external world, they are processed very much within this kind of enclosed space of reflection. And if that's the kind of poem I write most often, it's also the kind of poem that I usually feel most dissatisfied with.

There have been various projects that I have undertaken throughout my writing life which have been an attempt to move away from the occasional. Poems of research, like the verse-essay *Tracking Wildfire*,[1] where I want to break free of the spontaneity and the accidental nature of this receptiveness and susceptibility and work in a different way which requires a different kind of sustained concentration and engagement with the materials and is not dependent on some kind of Romantic mood settling on my head! So those are two different kinds of approaches to writing.

I wondered actually if it would be helpful to just point out in an older poem, 'Perpendicular Twins' in *Vacation of a Lifetime*,[2] a few things that went into this poem as a way of showing how, in what might seem to be an incredibly haphazard assemblage of found materials, where it actually comes from and what the unifying principles might be. Obviously with "the

---

[1] Andrea Brady, *Tracking Wildfire* (2007). The piece originally appeared on-line at dispatx.com, where it may still be viewed at: http://www.dispatx.com/show/item.php?item=2062. It was later republished in a print version—see footnote 36.

[2] Andrea Brady, *Vacation of a Lifetime* (Great Wilbraham: Salt Publishing, 2001), pp.52–53.

Talking Poetics

crisis over Kosovo"[3] there are references to very conspicuous international news events. "That one splits 31 boards over his head in 30 / seconds before the Texas viceregent / to reign over Regis"[4] in the second stanza, is a reference to Bush junior's first campaign. He was on the Regis Philbin talk show in America, following on from someone who was able to literally break boards over his head! And then moving on from there to an image of torture: "Needles of the latest various / thicknesses came to Uruguay / Benitez thought in the ambassador's pouch".[5] And then the "blue novelty of the Bell"[6] refers to a sign for a pub; this is also a road poem, picking up materials from the road, from travelling. In the next stanza "swelling started / in the leg like a sock of marbles",[7] that's actually from an interview with Stephen King I read, about how he'd had a terrible accident and broken his leg and it looked like a bag of marbles! And then the next stanza "the abridgement of memory / warden drives the last summer flock / through the ford into this homestead",[8] is a rewriting of 'Lycidas', which is one of the things I was engaging with quite intensely in the period when I was writing this poem, when I was doing my PhD thesis. So there's pastoral, but a rewriting of the pastoral and a distortion of the pastoral. "Can we ask Daniel the recipe / for a lump of pitch, fat and hairs to burst the snake",[9] was a translation I was doing in a Latin class of the Bible, talking about the biblical episode of Daniel the prophet.

So, you see, all of this stuff might seem as if it's just come out of my own imagination and yet it's all drawn from very specific sources, from textual and linguistic and material encounters that I was having at the time I was preparing to write this poem. And of course the twins that give the poem its title, that was another news story about conjoined twins and a debate about whether or not they ought to be separated in order that one could live and what was the moral case for that. So there are all these questions about proximity and pain, bodily pain, and bodily connectedness, as well as a kind of connectedness through the artery of

---

[3] Ibid., p. 52.
[4] Ibid., p. 52.
[5] Ibid., p. 52. See A.J. Langguth, *Hidden Terrors* (New York: Pantheon, 1978), p. 251, cited in Chomsky. Dan Mitrione, a security advisor for the CIA in Latin America, helped Uruguayan officials to secure the most up-to-date needles for use in torture, and trained security forces in their use.
[6] Ibid., p. 52.
[7] Ibid., p. 52.
[8] Ibid., p. 53.
[9] Ibid., p. 53.

the road, and of the physical landscape and forms of consciousness that are bursting apart as well as interpenetrating. That's how that poem came about. My husband has said that it seems that some of these poems are just quite random assemblages of objects, but that once he got to know me, he realised that actually they're drawn from very concrete and specific instances which are actually recoverable.

ST: So would this poem fit into the occasional category or would it be the alternative?

AB: For me, it would fit into the occasional category.

ST: Despite the fact that it's nevertheless ... I hesitate to use the word collage...

AB: I think that's a good word to use actually. Dadaist collage is something which has I think influenced my practice in some ways. It's important though to say that it's not a random assemblage.

It would fit into the occasional category for me because one of its orienting principles is personal and subjective experience. All of this material from the external world can narrow to a point around my own subjectivity. That's one of the disadvantages of the occasional poem for me, or one of its failings, which I try to exceed by working in these other modes.

ST: For me that openness to allowing other discourses to be present within the work would usually feel like that response to getting beyond occasionality, where one's resources might just be purely what one is capable of inventing on the spot. That's not to say that all of these things aren't available within a short proximity of time, because they can be, but they also seem for me like ways of extending the poem's scope already beyond the occasional.

AB: Well, I guess it's a question of the standards you hold yourself to in a way. For a reader it may look like extending beyond the personal and the intimate into the external world, but my concern is that it's actually the reverse: it's a bringing of the external world into the space of the personal in order to justify the attention to the personal. That's one thing that greatly concerns me and that I'm trying to work through—not to avoid, but to try to find the right kinds of ethical solutions to, in my work in general.

ST: I don't know how much you think of that issue of the personal in purely political terms, but here it seems to be leading aesthetic decisions in some way. Let's talk about how you revise.

AB: I guess for me, as for all poets, there is this very fragile balance between revision which improves and that which wrecks the original moment, the original poem. Especially for these poems which arise in moments of susceptibility. It's difficult afterwards to recreate that moment and the complex interplay of references and intuitions that goes into the movement of the text from one image or one found object to the next. And yet on the other hand there's also a desire in me to make my poems clearer. So revision will often entail unravelling some of the more compressed moments in the text and making them, if not exactly clear, then at least slightly more eligible for interpretation. So I don't tend to write more, I tend to take away when I'm revising, to cut rather than to enhance—the plastic surgery of revision!

ST: It's intriguing to hear you talk about this piece, because I remember in the online interview with Andrew Duncan[10] you also brought out some of the references going on in another poem in this book and it was very revealing. But I think what's interesting about it is that when one reads it, or for me at least, I get a sense of an argued set of relations—there's something about the way that you bring these things together that feels necessary, despite the fact that they are diverse. I don't know whether the ideal reading is that somebody does attempt to work out what the references are, because I'm not sure it would be really. Certainly not in the same way that *Tracking Wildfire* doesn't just ask you to follow those things but actually provides you with the material, although that's being constructed with a different set of intentions it seems to me.

AB: I think that if we regard instances of the kind which are catalogued in this poem, incidences of violence or of political oddity or of moral dilemmas that come up in public discourse, as local distortions which reflect much more general categories of relation, then in a way you don't need to know exactly what specific instances the poem refers to: it's not a kind of *poème à clef*, or allegory which finally reveals its single, shining meaning at the end. It's a kind of symptomotology of the way that general

---

[10] Andrew Duncan, 'Andrea Brady Interview', *The Argotist Online*. Viewable at: http://www.argotistonline.co.uk/Brady%20interview.htm

conditions of material production, of capital, of exploitation, of political organisation, and of human relatedness, manifest themselves within these ripples of strangeness or intensity that break through the barrier of a private consciousness and somehow seem to be, if not symbolic, then shiningly meaningful, or somehow emblematic or representative.

ST: So, in that sense, would it be fair to say it's a kind of miming of that informational chaos or does it have a critical element to it?

AB: Yeah, it does have a critical element, and also it's perhaps not chaotic in its attempt to order the intrusion of these kinds of information that none of us really know quite what to do with.

ST: So there's almost a kind of, I don't know if "managing" is the right word, but it seems to be trying to negotiate this territory in some way which somehow makes it graspable. Is that what becomes the occasion of the poem, to try and manage this set of circumstances in a way that's bearable?

AB: Yeah, that's a good way of putting it.

ST: I think one of the experiences of reading (and rereading) right through all of your work in one go was being struck by the way in which images were a recurrent device or technique. They are a very strong element in the writing almost to the point that I felt that there's an enabling tension in the work which is driven by that image-level thinking alongside other moments which sound like clearer attempts to articulate a particular position on something. The images can clearly originate from many different sources, and sometimes the image will be something that's seen, but I suppose it may also be something that's invented?

AB: I think that's right, that if the poems have morals, then the moral always comes afterwards, comes from the materiality of the language and of the images. It's that materiality which is assembled first, and it's only afterwards that I realise that there's any kind of figuration going on more generally (to put it in painterly terms).

We were talking about whether this might be influenced at all by John Wieners' work. I actually came to reading Wieners fairly late: I only started really seriously reading him maybe seven, eight years ago. So I think my way of working had already been established by then. One of the things I feel some sympathy for in Wieners' poetry is his capacity to use the image to transform what is sometimes really inexcusable melodrama or personal self-pity into something which transcends that moment. I admire Wieners' capacity to transfigure quite banal and self-absorbed reflections through moments of real particularity. For example, his 'A Poem for Trapped Things',[11] which is an extremely predictable and banal poem about a butterfly that's trapped in his room, I mean we can all guess the significance of that! But it ends with this image, he says something like "I watch you all day with my hand over my mouth"[12] and that's a strange and sudden shift of register and of intensity. You leave the realm of these slightly juvenile reflections on the symbol and so forth into a strange and unsettling image of a particular day and of a particular gesture. That's one of the things that I really admire in Wieners, he gets away with things that other poets really simply couldn't get away with. As my friend Daniel Kane always says, what other poet could write the lines: "It is so sad / It is so lonely".[13] It's just not excusable anymore!

In part my work is influenced by my study of early modern literature, and that, probably more than any of my contemporaries, is the source of this desire to unnerve the reader, for example by associating particular emotional or personal experiences, or physical sensations, or religious preoccupations with sudden alchemical, or geographical, or metallurgic metaphors and images. Donne is someone I've worked on a great deal, and George Herbert, Crashaw, Sir Thomas Browne, all used language in an extremely vivid and surprising way.

ST: When did you start writing?

AB: According to my family the first poem I ever wrote was a poem on the Lebanese hostage crisis in 1981 when I was six! We had an old nun, Sister Maureen, who had the TV on in our first grade classroom. I couldn't possibly understand the geopolitics of the situation but I knew we were meant to be praying for the Americans! I wrote a poem in rhyming couplets about, please God, send them home safely!

---

[11] John Wieners, 'A Poem for Trapped Things' from *Ace of Pentacles* (1964). See *Selected Poems 1958–1984*, ed. by Raymond Foye (Santa Barbara, CA: Black Sparrow Press, 1986), p. 57.
[12] "I watch you / all morning / long. / With my hand over my mouth". Ibid., p. 57.
[13] John Wieners, 'The Loneliness' in Wieners, *Cultural Affairs in Boston: Poetry and Prose 1956–1985* (Santa Rosa, CA: Black Sparrow, 1988), p. 131.

Andrea Brady

ST: How did moving to the UK change the way you work?

AB: I've been writing my whole life, but, like most people, the poetry that I was exposed to when I was at school culminated in high modernism with its melancholia and its morbidity. It gave me the sense that to be a serious poet you have to have the cadences and the despair of Eliot or someone like that. It was when I went to Columbia as an undergraduate and took some courses with Kenneth Koch and ended up working quite closely with him, that I was exposed to, not only the work of the New York School—Koch gave me my copy of the collected poems of Frank O'Hara, which had just come out at that point, as well as all of his own work—but also this incredible range of writing in translation and so forth that I had never encountered before, stuff that Koch was very influenced by and liked a great deal, Pasternak and Mayakovsky for example. Koch was constantly trying to get me and my writing to be more joyful and more liberated! I guess it's the usual story of going away to college isn't it, from my old girls' catholic high school with the nuns, to the sudden divergence and hedonism of New York City and Columbia and being free!

So, when I came to Cambridge—I did my junior year abroad there—I was introduced to the work of J.H. Prynne, which really carried the banner of high modernism's seriousness and difficulty. I felt intellectually very turned on by it and also inspired by the beauty and lyricism of some of Prynne's earlier work and also drawn, perhaps just by temperament, to its linguistic complexity. And so then when I went back to Columbia and ran into Koch again, there was this controversy between us about seriousness versus lightness, or the dour English influences versus the lightness and the happiness of a New York poetry. And then I came back to England again and eventually settled here permanently. I think O'Hara is definitely one of the poets, if not close to the poet, for whom I have the greatest admiration and love. I really love his poetry; I feel I know it by heart. But it's difficult sometimes to reconcile O'Hara to the climate and conditions of England, and certainly of Cambridge where I ended up.

I think that struggle is also in evidence in some of the work, especially in *Vacation of a Lifetime*, in the section 'The Torpedo of Excess'. A lot of those poems are about negotiating between these two very different environments, bringing my family history and personal history into a situation of extraordinary intellectual and romantic intensity, right at the colonial centre. These issues are at the heart of the poem 'Function of the Commonwealth and Overseas Trust'.[14] I was under the auspices of the Commonwealth and Overseas Trust as a postgraduate student, and I went to one of their garden parties and there we were, all the former colonials, encouraged to wear our national dress, eating our canapés, and Prince Charles was there! Going from a situation where you grow up believing yourself to be a citizen of the country which is both the most powerful and really the centre of the world, to suddenly finding yourself in the midst of an old order in which you're out of place, uncouth and almost illiterate, was very strange for me and obviously brought up a lot of conflicts. Some of that is articulated in the poetry of that time as well.

ST: That's really fascinating! Do you think of yourself as a British writer?

AB: [Laughter] I don't think of myself as an American one!

ST: That's the other question implicit.

AB: I don't think of myself as a British writer, not really. I carry an American passport, but the situation in America, the aesthetic one, is totally unfamiliar to me. Also the grass roots level references—I feel not only alienated by but also ignorant of that culture, the popular culture of the States which would be the material of my poetry if I lived there. So there's a sense of strange homelessness and unfamiliarity when I go there. But I wouldn't want to elevate that homelessness to the condition of other kinds of modernist experimentation, to claim to be homeless everywhere—I think I'm much too fat and settled for that.

What's more strange for me is the way that I'm often labelled a Cambridge poet, which is not a label which makes sense to me in any number of ways. In terms of the *Chicago Review* controversy between John Wilkinson and Peter Riley, one of the questions that Andrew Duncan's letter raised was whether I belong in the genealogy of the Cambridge poets. I'm not sure that I do really. Andrew was commenting on Peter and John Wilkinson's attempt to negotiate the Cambridge school past and present, and if there is such a thing and who belongs to it and what belongs to it as well.

ST: Let's take on this thorny word "innovation", because it is something which is nailed to the masthead of my research bid, for better or for worse, and I'm almost contractually obliged to ask you about it! I'd be interested in

---

[14] Brady, *Vacation of a Lifetime*, p. 60.

what it means to you in relation to your own writing, and to contemporary poetry in more general terms. I've offered a sense of where I think it's going which seems to make it increasingly difficult to use it in the way that I'd got used to, to the point that I took it for granted really. But might we also explore whether it—aside from this particular context of usage—really speaks to us as a concept that is necessary in some way?

AB: I think like you that it's a term which I used to use much more comfortably than I could do now. I was just noticing that it formed part of my description of the Archive of the Now in a conversation I had with Rosheen Brennan, which was published on *How2*.[15] At that point it seemed like the most acceptable way of designating this late Modernist, or experimental or avant-garde work or whatever else you want to call it! But now my encounter with the term innovation is almost entirely in the context of institutions, in my case the academic sector, where it is a perpetual requirement to show that we are innovating, mostly for the sake of innovating. And it's a term which seems to have enormous government inertia behind it. There's so much pressure to show how you are revolutionising your field or your own job description or whatever, just as a way of proving that you're not stuck in old ways of working. So it's about the expansion of the economy and the creative industries. It's a term which also seems to come very much from scientific and industrial management. So it's really problematic. It suggests too that a constant forward motion is the only thing which is required; there's no necessity for reflection on the past and no recognition that present ways of working might actually be acceptable, or even more than acceptable, that they might be the best ways of working. That's my problem with the term innovation!

And then there's Adorno's critique of the culture industry as replicating innovation at the level of technique and form in order to disguise the fact that content, and also the needs that the culture industry serves, never actually change. There's an illusion of transformation at a technical level but not true transformation at the level of the base. That's another reason I would be suspicious of the term.

ST: Is it more useful just to point to a tradition or a history of work, more than an actual property of it in a sense?

---

[15] 'Andrea Brady in conversation with Rosheen Brennan', *How2*, vol. 3, no. 1 (Summer 2007). Viewable at: http://www.asu.edu/pipercwcenter/how2journal/vol_3_no_1/new_media/archive_ofthe_now/pdfs/bradyinterview.pdf

AB: Is that the way it's used now?

ST: That's where we've got to with the journal at least.[16] After much soul-searching, it was just, it's got to be that, anything else is going to be even more problematic.

AB: I suppose that's right, it's the least bad alternative. I've never liked the term experimental because it means that there's a kind of provisionality about the work, as if it's only a mechanism of discovering another truth which is exterior to it. And the term avant-garde doesn't seem very appropriate either, in part because it suggests a kind of cohesiveness of groups with manifestoes that meet regularly and have commonalities and I don't think, unfortunately, any of those properties really apply to our little community. And avant-garde, well it just sounds a little bit ridiculous. I don't think we deserve its militancy either, unfortunately.

ST: What about Ron Silliman's term the post-avant which has hit these shores in a big way recently?

AB: Oh, I'm so tired of being post-everything! I don't feel postmodern. There is an exhibition at the Tate called Alter-modern or something, which claims we're also post-postmodern.[17] Or we're identified as the "radical tradition", which is an even more transparent attempt to associate artists with political revolutionaries. There are significant problems with all the terms that we come up with. But it's interesting that it should be so

---

[16] A reference to my co-editorship (with Robert Sheppard) of the *Journal of British and Irish Innovative Poetry* (2009–).

[17] "A new modernity is emerging, reconfigured to an age of globalisation—understood in its economic, political and cultural aspects: an altermodern culture. Increased communication, travel and migration are affecting the way we live. Our daily lives consist of journeys in a chaotic and teeming universe. Multiculturalism and identity is being overtaken by creolisation: Artists are now starting from a globalised state of culture. This new universalism is based on translations, subtitling and generalised dubbing. Today's art explores the bonds that text and image, time and space, weave between themselves. Artists are responding to a new globalised perception. They traverse a cultural landscape saturated with signs and create new pathways between multiple formats of expression and communication. The Tate Triennial 2009 at Tate Britain presents a collective discussion around this premise that postmodernism is coming to an end, and we are experiencing the emergence of a global altermodernity". Nicolas Bourriaud, 'Altermodern Manifesto: Postmodernism is Dead' (Tate Britain, 2009). Viewable at: http://www.tate.org.uk/britain/exhibitions/altermodern/

problematic because I think it's a reminder of our desire for a cohesiveness that is recognisable within literary history while it's happening, and a desire for continuity that substantiates or elevates our efforts, continuity with Modernism, with twentieth-century avant-garde traditions and so forth. We'd like to think that we are the inheritors of those potentials. But at the same time it's a recognition that there isn't that cohesiveness, and that the work perhaps does deservedly occupy this space within a kind of managerial framework for the creative industries. It's enabled by that framework and it's enabled by the academic institutions in which so many of us work.

ST: As you've mentioned Adorno, to what extent does your political thinking and your writing come from Adorno and others in that tradition of thought?

AB: Adorno's another writer who I first encountered at Columbia, when I was taking a class on the Frankfurt School with Andreas Huyssen, and who immediately had an enormous, profound effect on me, even though I really didn't understand it as much as I should have! I think that Adorno's critique of the culture industry is still extremely pertinent to the way that we all find ourselves working. The attempt to analyse social and cultural phenomena with reference both to the possibilities for transcendence in thought and with reference to the economic base of production seems to me accurate and necessary, essential, vital. But one of the things which is most important for me about Adorno, and which has only become clear as I've matured as a reader of his work, is the space which is left within his philosophy—despite its incredibly intense rigours and its negativity—for transformation, for happiness. Despite the torn halves which don't add up, despite the negative dialectic which rolls on, crushing everything in its path, that there is a kind of glimmer of an alternative. And the recognition that happiness can be glimpsed within culture even though that potential for happiness cannot be realised until it is generally realisable, is one which has completely informed my poetry. Adorno reveals the dialectical relationship between the autonomy and the apparent or illusory freedoms of high culture, and the general condition; but also the sense that culture nonetheless can show us a way through to something different, even though that offer is also contaminated and imprisoned by the conditions which produce culture in the first place. The fact that I live this incredibly bourgeois life in which I'm paid to work on literature enables me to write poems in which I have the time to seriously consider the potential for freedom and happiness. But that potential for freedom and happiness is only ever going to be achieved if people like me no longer exist because the whole sphere of labour has been radically transformed.

ST: A question I had in store is closer to Adorno than I'd realised, in that it was about the way you're negotiating happiness, possibility, love and hope, they're all terms that you've used. It seems natural to jump forward to that. Ultimately I find Adorno's poetics impossible to ignore, but it's a very tough position to take on as a writer sometimes: that the most one can hope for is possibility, a glimpse of something, rather than something that could actually be realised, or is realised at any level. I still don't feel I can argue with it, but I want to!

AB: I'm not aware of anywhere in Adorno's thinking where very private and personal, intimate or family relationships are described in any depth, although reflections on the domestic and private do come into *Minima Moralia*, for example. The private and the personal are places which I'm interested in investigating for the potential conditions for happiness. Of course, Adorno does recognise in language and art what I think he refers to as the "coercionless synthesis of a manifold".[18] that there is something in the model of language and art for relations which are not entirely free of violence or appropriation but are also not entirely soaked through with those. So I think you're right, I think that Adorno's critique is impossible to ignore.

ST: It seems to be that those questions are the ones that are very much preoccupying you in the most recent work. Presumably when you did the interview with Andrew you were in the process of writing it [**AB**: Yes.] because you framed it as this question of "how to be faithful without misrecognising ironic self-entrapment as commitment, how to escape the mourning attitude"[19] and I felt that that was a really powerful statement of intent for that work. I was wondering how you feel the work has answered that question, if it has.

AB: I think there's been a gradual movement along the spectrum for me from the question of ethics in *Liberties* and the testing of virtue, through much more public engagements with the situation of the American,

---

[18] See Simon Jarvis, *Adorno: A Critical Introduction* (Cambridge: Polity Press, 1998), p.32.
[19] Duncan, 'Andrea Brady Interview', op. cit.

Western consumer and citizen—the work of the middle period! Recently, yes, I have been trying to engage with the ethics of happiness. I think it's much more difficult to write about happiness and from the position of happiness than it is to write from a position of sorrow and mourning and anger because, whilst sorrow can always be projected onto the whole population, happiness can't be. So happiness feels like an indulgence of a private attitude which ought not to interest anyone, whereas misery can elevate the personal into a universal condition. And yet, when you go back and you read Plato and Aristotle, they declare that happiness is the end of all politics, the pursuit of happiness is the aim and the goal of all political arrangements. It has an incredibly dense political meaning and history.

So I've been trying to write about being happy. In recent months since Ayla was born, that has emerged in a series of prose reflections on home and on her as an individual and also as a special case of the human! When she was born I started writing these notes, with datelines. They were not in any way meant to be a journal, but as kind of a record of her development and her emergence into the world and my understanding of her. And I wrote them in part because I was too tired for anything else! I was just too beat for poetry and I thought this material is too good, it's too important for me to pass up and I don't want to forget it. And so I tried to stay within the immediacy of the moments of her life and just detail them as we went along as a family. And in a way that work, which is very prosaic and extremely clear, is just a sort of portraiture of a person who, because she can't walk yet, is kind enough to stay still and be scrutinised! I wasn't sure if I was taking notes towards the work, or if it was the work, or if it was about the work and the poetic work was really the work of relatedness that we were doing on that rug right there with those toys. But now I've performed it three times at readings and people have responded very enthusiastically to it, so I've already kind of violated the privacy of these notes and made them public, which transforms the situation of that writing. It's no longer just private drafts towards something which might be produced later on, which presumably would have all the caveats and defences of the other work that we've been looking at—it's been made public.

It's been incredibly interesting actually in thinking about this interview to go back and read *Liberties* again, which is a text that I had avoided for a long time because I regarded it as embarrassing juvenilia—like a picture of me with my skirt tucked into my knickers! I didn't really want to have to relive all those moments. But actually now enough time has passed, I can see some of the strengths and advantages of that work. I almost feel as if I've come full-circle. In *Liberties* I was trying to write very much about personal virtue and personal relations and I was still young enough and self-absorbed enough to feel that that was legitimate and could interest readers. The poems I think have a kind of, well, "charming quality" makes them sound trivial, but they have a kind of sincerity and clarity and truthfulness about them which then the work lost for a while. And I feel that now, because I'm writing about Ayla and my love for her and about the phenomenology of infancy and her experience of her body, or what I can discern of it anyway, I feel that I'm returning to that slightly naive idiom, where those defences against private pronouncements within a public space have actually crumbled away a little bit. So it's an interesting kind of circuit.

ST: I had no idea you were writing such things! Are they out somewhere?

AB: No, they're not really out anywhere and I don't know if I'll publish them either. I still don't know what's going to happen to this book. I thought originally, well maybe I could give it to Ayla when she grows up. But then I thought, what would my response be to receiving a text like this from my mother? It would be incredibly moving, but it would also be overwhelming and embarrassing, because it is a depiction of this excruciatingly intense intimacy. The physical intimacy between the mother and the infant, of that bond, is almost impossible to imagine unless you're in the middle of experiencing it. Even after you've had a child of your own, it's very hard to put yourself in that place, the place of the infant. That's part of the work of the poems, to try to think myself into and through her. But perhaps she'll feel she doesn't want my minute reflections on her, filling up the blissful ignorance of her own past, that the oblivion of her infancy should stay empty and stay hers. So I don't know what it would be like to receive it as a gift. Maybe once she had her own children she would sympathise with it a little bit more.

ST: There could be a process of feeling differently about it at different times. [**AB**: Yeah.] It's fascinating because it somehow makes a connection between part of what drew me to thinking about Jennifer's work in the way that she's followed a particular path with her poetry writing and then wrote this huge autobiography which is addressing the reader in a very different way.

AB: Yeah, but which in a way is also conventional autobiography: it's not just about her most private moments, it's also a contextualisation of her work and a discussion of the various social settings in which she was writing which is extremely helpful to readers of her poetry and also to people who are interested in those poetry "scenes". One of the things that makes me uneasy about this prose work I've been doing, is that it is incredibly introverted. I mean really it is about the things that happen within the four walls of this house. It's much more narcissistic and perhaps much more dull than something which takes in the celebrities of the San Diego poetry scene!

ST: But could there be a positive narcissism in which that attention—which I don't think is only to yourself, from what you're saying—is quite legitimate to explore? Psychologically there are notions of positive and negative narcissism which give alternative ways in which it can develop.[20]

AB: Yes, well I think that's true. In the case of these prose notes, it isn't just about me, it is also an attempt to write a phenomenology of infancy. When I was pregnant, and then when I had just had Ayla, I was trying to find texts about infants to help me think through what I was experiencing, and there just really wasn't that much out there. This anthology that Cathy Wagner edited I found very useful but I only came across it recently.[21]

Most of the other work I found about infants fell into one or two categories. One of which was Romantic reflections on the sleeping babe over there who allows me to recollect my own youth or idealise the baby's life and upbringing. That tradition seemed to me quite self-absorbed: the infant was just a reflection of the parents' wishes and memories. And then on the other hand, there were women writing about the difficulties, the trials of motherhood and how it diverted them from their work and changed their sense of their own identity, and about the losses associated with motherhood. But there weren't that many specific poetic portraits of the child. I found that really interesting. (Maybe Alice Notley's poems would be one notable exception.)

As I sit and watch Ayla, suddenly over the course of an afternoon she realizes that if she waves her hand she can make this octopus that's

---

[20] See Harald Walach, 'Narcissism—The shadow of transpersonal psychology' in *Transpersonal Psychology Review*, vol. 12, no. 2 (2008), 47–57.
[21] *Not for Mothers Only: Contemporary Poems on Child-getting and Child-rearing*, ed. by Catherine Wagner and Rebecca Wolff (Albany NY: Fence Books, 2007).

dangling above her move, and suddenly discover then that she has a hand and that her body can cause effects within the material world that she finds herself in. What could be more profound than that? So Ayla is a special case of the human condition or an experiment in the uncovery of the ontic or whatever! And being with her allows me to see in practice all those aspects of our encounters with the world, with concepts and sound and movement, which we read about in books, but absolutely at their foundation. But whereas the philosophers' *cogito* is always a grown man, infantilised by doubt or bracketing or whatever, I feel like I'm watching her build up her moral and cognitive universe completely from scratch. It's just really fascinating, all of the insights she's given me into language and communication and the way that categories are discovered, categories of matter or of relation. So yeah, it's not just about me as mum, how I cope with that: it's mostly about her.

ST: So are you drawing on writings about infant development?

AB: Yes, textbooks on child development are the things which I found most interesting, on the development of the brain, or of language or the different kinds of concepts they develop and at what stages. Actually being able to monitor her progress through those stages has been really interesting.

ST: Extraordinary. This writing that you're doing is so unexpected! I had a question about risk-taking which could in some way connect with this work?

AB: I think we've touched on it a few times. When I first saw that question, I was thinking, well, it would be really a self-valorising exaggeration to say that anything that I do is risky. Everything is accommodated within the over-studied field of late Modernist literary production. There's nothing that can really be particularly adventurous. One of the things that I experience as a risk from the supply side, is this negotiation between the personal and the public, and whether by attaching my own private ideas and reflections and experiences with tiny hooks onto public discourse, news events and so forth, I'm actually exploiting other people's suffering or disadvantage in order to aggrandise my own work. That is the ethical predicament of all of my work. One of the risks I suppose would be to become so absorbed within that predicament that you either don't do anything or you become obsessed with it and incapable of actually trying to push beyond it.

ST: I don't know whether you felt that you'd reached a point where that was the case, it still seems to me that there's a shift in the new work that I'm calling *Presenting*.²² But certainly with the work you're describing now, that seems to be something altogether different.

AB: When I've performed this recent prose work I have felt the risk that it will be misunderstood, and I haven't really experienced that fear before. Generally I think the potential for misunderstanding is written into the germ-line of my poems, and I'm quite happy with that. Also the potential for understandings which are more complex than the material in the first place, which is always a bonus! But I don't want the work I'm doing now to be misunderstood as somehow implying that there's some essential connection between being a woman and being a mother and being a writer, or that I have any privileged insight into the human condition just because I have spent some time looking after a baby. But inevitably I think the experience of pregnancy and childbirth is an enormous shock and revelation, and certainly it has made me reconsider some of my ideas about mutuality and autonomy. One of the things I keep coming back to in my poems about pregnancy and childbirth is that, if this were an experience which could be taken as a radical base for communal organisation, then communities would look quite different than they do now. Western selfhood and legalistic and philosophical conceptions of subjecthood seem to be premised entirely on preserving an idea of autonomy. And yet, being split into two people in a condition of extraordinary pain and generosity, of physical generosity, is a revelation of a different kind of mutuality that I could never have suspected, even though of course I know the facts about the birds and the bees! So I think this work in that sense is deeply political, not just because the personal is political and we know that the conditions of women in the domestic sphere are political conditions, but because it is produced from a situation which presents the most enormous and profound challenge to ideas of independence and autonomy.

ST: That's utterly fascinating. To return to *Liberties* for a moment, and you spoke earlier about Milton in relation to that book, I was detecting some elements of seventeenth-century poetics. At what point did that start as a project?

---

[22] The working title of Andrea's latest manuscript at the time of the interview. Now entitled *The Rushes*, it is due to be published by Reality Street in 2011/12.

Talking Poetics

AB: It started when I lived in Boston for a year, and then when I went back to Cambridge it gained some momentum. It did draw on some of the early modern texts I was reading, and also on this ancient and idyllic landscape in Cambridge. When I think of the spaces in the poem I often think of the Grantchester Meadows outside of Cambridge. There's this image of rape that recurs in the poem and partially that's oil seed rape, the yellow livid crop which acts as a border or a boundary to the fields where people walk for recreation.

ST: Ok, understood in that sense. It's even on the cover of one of Keston's books,[23] isn't it? It seemed to be like a trope that was in the air at one point.

AB: Yeah. Rape, of course, in both senses, also in the sense of a violent predation. You picked up that whiteness is a recurrent trope in the book: it's there in the opening epigraph from Milton's *Areopagitica*. Whiteness, as I think John Hall wrote, is every colour in light and no colour in pigment, so it already has this strange oppositional character, and one of the things that the sequence is interested in exploring is a desire to be, I think I say at one point, "beyond reproach",[24] but also to be tested. It's a sequence about personal ethics within a pastoral setting, worked through tropes about personal intimacy and sexual love, where whiteness represents a sort of blankness. In Milton's argument, virtue which isn't tested becomes just an excremental whiteness, something which is external or a kind of sloughing off: the strange double entendre of "excremental". So it's about virtue and about testing and that's in part where the rape topos comes in. Think of all these women who put themselves on the line in various Renaissance pastorals and end up getting raped or nearly raped, because their virtue and their innocence is exposed within these arcadias which are places where masculine virtue and heroism can be displayed but so can their contrary—barbaric, rough masculinities associated with nature. It's about a willingness to expose oneself to violence and viciousness and to see what can be constructed out of that exposure.

The title *Liberties* also reflects that, in that the Liberties were the district which was beyond the law, beyond civic jurisdiction, where entertainment and theatres and bear-baiting and prostitution took place. So the pastoral,

---

[23] Keston Sutherland, *Antifreeze* (Cambridge: Barque Press, 2002).
[24] Brady, *Vacation of a Lifetime*, p. 34. The phrase in context of section 16 of 'Liberties: the City Adorned like a Bride' *Part 2* reads: "You call in sick, you re-opened your grazes, slid in / to escape reproach, and wish still to be beyond reproach / to lie in deep grass".

but also the verges of the city where the raucousness and the sexual licence of a real pleasure garden could exist, that space now being cancelled and moved into the jurisdiction of the culture industry. In those poems I was thinking about personal ethics and exposure of virtue to vice, to testing. I tried to create a dialectical structure, in that many of the poems vacillate between reproach or complaint and then a desire for closeness and intimacy. That partially is a reflection of the relationship I was in at the time and this kind of violent struggle between love and enmity. The book ends with a desire for paradise which is finally articulated but then is shut off. So I've got 'Lycidas', *Areopagitica* and *Paradise Lost* all in one concise sequence!

Now when I look at it and I read 'Pornopolis', which is the first poem of the next section of *Vacation of a Lifetime*, it's a real refutation of this attempt to test virtue and vice through sexual intimacy that was happening in the first poem. It's almost a parody of that. Pornopolis is a character in the neo-Latin closet drama *Christus triumphans* by the martyrologist John Foxe.[25] Pornopolis is also the city which is wedded to pornographic sexual desires, Babylon essentially. So we go from the "City Adorned like a Bride" which is a description of Jerusalem from the Book of Revelation, to the whore of Babylon, the city of lust and sexual depravity. It feels a bit tragic to me, this arc from a kind of testing—but one which is very much wrapped up in a personal ethics rather than in a quest for justice—into this satiric or ironic position. But it develops into an attempt I think eventually to move out of this ironic position into a search for a public justice that can engage with personal suffering, but which has had to disavow the personal in order to get there.

ST: So that's what is happening throughout 'The Torpedo of Excess'?

AB: Yeah. I think the tone of that sequence, well it's not a sequence, of those poems is much more jaded and sarcastic and it doesn't really allow itself to claim any unalloyed joy and pleasure. Instead of the sexual intimacy and love which is chronicled in *Liberties* you have many characters who are hermaphroditic sexual performers in it.

ST: It's pretty hair-raising stuff! That term "excess" is something that my attention's called to in a different way now that John's subtitled his collection of essays "the poetry of excess".[26] What further resonance does it

---

[25] 1517–1587
[26] John Wilkinson, *The Lyric Touch: Essays on the Poetry of Excess* (Great Wilbraham: Salt Publishing, 2007).

have? Obviously within the context of what you've just been describing that seems to be quite specific, and also perhaps refers to the kind of opening to the range of discourses that is going on here.

AB: The title of 'The Torpedo of Excess' comes from a seventeenth-century translation by Edward Sherburne of Seneca, where he talks about being "benumbed by the torpedo of excess".[27] I'll read a bit of it:

> Be not possest with Terror of those things,
> Which Gods apply as the Minds spurs, not stings.
> Misfortune's vertues Opportunity.
> All men those wretched thinke deservedly,
> Who languish on the bed of Happinesse,
> Benum'd with the Torpedo of Excesse.
> Whom dull Tranquility, and stupid ease,
> Detaine like Vessells in becalmed Seas.
> What e're to such befalls, will strange appeare;
> Men unexperienc'd, Crosses hardly beare.

Misfortune is an opportunity, and happiness is a kind of lasciviousness whose effect is comparable to the stingray (that's the meaning of "torpedo" in this period). So there's this kind of doubleness in my use of the term: the torpedo of excess is soporific and enervating, and excess and happiness and indulgence make us numb and incapable of carrying the crosses which are actually our opportunities to prove our virtue, picking up that theme from the first collection. But then also the torpedo as we know it, is that which could blow the thing apart. So is the poetry that excessive language use which actually numbs you in some ways, and whose over-indulgence makes you incapable of acting more deliberately in the world? Or is it that which blows apart the excesses of a consumer society? I think the book and the poetry in general are always trying to test those two related potential needs for excess, on the one hand the excess of consumption and on the other the excess of production, of poetic production specifically.

ST: That really helps me to understand the logic of development in those works. I think I sensed it in some way but it's really useful to get your take on it.

---

[27] Edward Sherburne, trans., *Seneca's answer to Lucilius his quaere why good men suffer misfortunes seeing there is a divine providence?* (London, 1648), p. 18.

AB: I was saying before that it's partially also about being in Cambridge and being out of place there and being confronted by this extremely conservative, patriarchal set of institutions. In that case the desire to prove oneself and to explore how personal intimacy could lead to a kind of personal ethic actually hits, not a brick wall, but a nicely stone-masoned wall with mullioned windows! And the outcome is a series of poems which are confrontational but exaggerated too in their performance of, especially, sexual resistance. So that's why I would say that poems like 'Girl Talk'[28] aren't really informed necessarily by Wieners.

ST: Yeah, because you weren't reading him at the time.

AB: No, but maybe that signals why I felt I had a particular affinity to Wieners when I came across him in terms of that performance of resistance and difference.

ST: Do you think you were picking up on his influence through the writers you were reading, sort of by proxy almost?

AB: Wilkinson would be the only person who I was reading who was conspicuously influenced by him. But of course I was reading O'Hara a great deal at the time.

ST: So that covers three quarters of the book, *Liberties* is presented as two sections, but you've been talking about it with 'The Torpedo of Excess' as one ongoing, complete project.

AB: Yeah, I think the second section of poems was very much written in response to the first, and it was all revised together.

ST: I remember reading this on the internet I think, was that its first appearance?

AB: Yeah, on Brian Kim Stefans' website.[29] They were very different versions.

ST: Then it moves into what does feel perhaps more like a sequence towards the end of the book, the 'Seasonals'. I think it's a great device and it works extremely well, to choose those holidays as sites for poems to work on. I wonder if you could say how they came about and how they fit into the unfolding logic of this book as you're describing it?

---

[28] Brady, *Vacation of a Lifetime*, p. 61.
[29] The Arras webzine, archived at: www.arras.net/

AB: Part of my maturation from my girlhood into becoming independent as a person and as a writer, also included a sloughing off of the Catholicism that I grew up with. But one of the things which I missed a great deal was the liturgical year, the seasons marked by ritual observances that brought a community together in observation and anticipation. And there was nothing like that left for me. So I decided I wanted to write a series of seasonal poems to think about how civic holidays and festivities were moments of convergence for the community, and to think about their history and also ways in which they've been emptied out in modern life. So that was an attempt to find some way of synthesising individual but not necessarily private experiences with more communal experiences, without the overwhelmingly vicious irony that was present in the intermediate work. And it also was an opportunity for thinking about how specific events in the news cycle could be integrated into natural history and our estrangement from the land and agrarian cycles.

ST: Can you give an example of that tension between natural history and current affairs?

AB: In 'Britain reciprocate Zimbabwe: another Easter seasonal 0j'[30] I was thinking about the conflict between Britain and Zimbabwe and Mugabe, and about Easter as a festival of renewal and rebirth, and the Spring and the pagan aspects of the history of paschal ceremony. And thinking about the agricultural produce that comes to Sainsbury's from places like Zimbabwe, and about how the seasons are inverted in the northern and southern hemispheres and so Easter takes place in Autumn, in a time of decay and gathering rather than of sowing. That poem also incorporates some references to a trip that Keston and I took to South Africa and Namibia in, it must have been 1999, which I think had a really profound effect on both of us.

ST: Is that where you are on the cover? There're these little photographs.

AB: I think that's in the Lake District actually!

ST: It doesn't look very African but who knows?! The word "information" seems quite a charged term through these poems and links back to what you've just been saying about negotiating the kinds of material that were available to you through various new media.

---
[30] Brady, *Vacation of a Lifetime*, p. 113.

AB: Yeah, the intrusion of information as well as the managed flow of information through us as literary professionals, as critics and writers.

ST: I was thinking about Douglas Oliver and his response to Africa. In 'May Day/ok' you've got "nubian woman" and "gazelle flesh", images which also suggest Africa to me.[31]

AB: Yeah, that was very much about reproduction. We were talking before about how my new work has been inspired by having a child, but I think the possibility of eventually having a child is something that's preoccupied me in a lot of other poems as well. Another element of this trajectory from a sexual trial in the earlier poems through a slightly camp sexual performance in the intermediate work is then also trying to eventually work out questions about fecundity and reproduction and sexuality which actually have a living outcome in my most recent poems.

I read *A Salvo for Africa* and I did write about it in *Quid*.[32] I think I was more generous to it in that review than in retrospect I would say the poem really deserved, because I don't think it is a successful set of poems, but I very much admired the spirit of it.

ST: I agree. I'm also noting how that logic you've just been unfolding reminds me of what Caroline's doing in her *Goan Atom* project where the first section is called 'Doll' and then it moves onto 'Bride'. I don't want to make too obvious a comparison but there is a structural logic of a gendered aspect to development running through that.

AB: Yeah. Those of us who grew up Catholic have a coming-of-age ritual when you're about seven, first communion, where you are a bride of Christ, and you get all dressed up in your white dress with the veil.

ST: I've seen the photographs of my wife going through all this.

AB: Christ and I needed to get a divorce!

ST: Changing tack again, I wanted to ask you more about the trope of twins, which you mentioned earlier. It's there in some of John Wilkinson's stuff, and you were talking about it through Gillian Rose's work, where she

---

[31] Ibid., p. 115.
[32] Andrea Brady, 'Review of Douglas Oliver *A Salvo for Africa*' (2000), *Quid* 4 (2000), 19–20. Viewable at http://www.barquepress.com/quid4.pdf

uses it as a figure for otherness, in your piece on Kevin Nolan's book.[33] It is also there in *Vacation*, and you've explained that more straightforwardly in terms of a story about conjoined twins. But I don't know how it's operating in *Cold Calling*.

AB: I think that again was another case where conjoined twins were in the news. I think for Wilkinson one of the interests of twins is twin-speak, that there is a kind of idiolect, a private language shared between twins. It's a very interesting idea, but it's not something I've thought about very carefully. I didn't realise it came up as a trope in my work [**ST**: Well, localised.] but if it does it's probably just because it's another special case of a bond between two individuals and working out the energies and dynamics of that. The idea of conjoined twins in particular ties into some of the things I was saying before about autonomy. In this case it's an extreme physical example of heteronomy, that you're actually pulled in a different direction by a body which is partly you and is partly not you.

ST: I've got a note here: "ok, conjoined twins"! Maybe it's not such a leap from there to reflect on how pronouns function in your work. Clearly they are a conspicuous part of speech in the way they operate in your poems, and the way the second person functions, particularly the way the word "she" functions, the way that "I" functions, all of these feel under a lot of pressure within the writing. This is now shifting the focus to *Embrace*, passages like the lines in 'All or Nothing': "Was I right , was I […] / if I gave up my own tongue, I for that matter",[34] and this section towards the end of 'Building Site' where "you" and "yours" build up quite a strong effect.[35] I know it's just part of the material we have to use as writers, but I wonder if you had any thoughts or comments on that?

AB: I guess I can admit that the first section of *Liberties*, 'The White Wish', all of the "she"s were originally "I"s. There's obviously a desire for a psychic distancing that goes with the movement away from I and towards she. And yet, whilst "she" is probably the most appropriate of the third-person pronouns to apply to myself, it is like unexploded ordnance in the poem. There's no way that that sequence would have made sense, in the sense of

---

[33] Andrea Brady, 'Now is the Night: Notes on Kevin Nolan's *Elegiac Doubles*' in *Necessary Steps: Poetry, Elegy, Walking, Spirit*, ed. David Kennedy (Exeter: Shearsman Books, 2007), pp. 11–27.
[34] Andrea Brady, *Embrace* (Glasgow: Object Permanence, 2005), pp. 48–49.
[35] Ibid., p. 19.

the testing and the sexual exposure, if I had had "he"; and yet writing "she" does seem to be a gesture which calls attention to itself, attention of a very particular kind, which is sometimes unwelcome attention as well.

I'm also reluctant to give up the I, and I'm reluctant to give up the personal address of the you as well, because these poems aren't simply pronouncements into the ether, or deluded senatorial addresses to the whole of humanity, they are often imagined dialogues with specific people, and dialogues which I hope are worth overhearing.

There is a great deal of poetry in which, because process has been foregrounded or because the strain of relations under capitalism are being investigated, personhood slips away almost entirely. I think poems of that sort, for me personally, cede too much ground. I can imagine a great deal in my diagnosis of exploitation but one thing I can't imagine is not having a body, not having a self. Relations pass through us as individuals, and I think you can't simply take yourself out of that equation, out of that matrix, and represent the relations as somehow subsisting independently amongst themselves. I guess that officially disqualifies me from being postmodern! But again I'm very aware of how self-absorbed these pronouns may make the poems seem, in the way we've been talking about before.

ST: I'm not sure that's quite the effect as such, because they do feel contested and problematised at every turn, but in that way they do acquire a real weight, that they're worth fighting for in some sense. I want to make a link between *Embrace* and *Tracking Wildfire*, but first I must admit that the way that I've been thinking about *Tracking Wildfire* is very much as a poem rather than as a "verse essay". I even had to print it!

AB: Well, I'm trying to get it published! Because I think the experience of reading it on the page would be quite different.[36]

ST: I did have the experience of working it with on the screen as well, that was my primary experience of it, but I wanted to get closer to it so I cut and pasted it and it eventually allowed me to put it in some form that I could then print. But it does show where the highlighted texts were. That's great if it will appear.

AB: I don't know if it will appear, I'm trying to get someone to do it. I do

---

[36] After the interview took place the text appeared in print as *Wildfire: A Verse Essay on Obscurity and Illumination* (San Francisco: Krupskaya, 2010). Further references in the interview are to this edition.

think there are advantages to working in that hypertext format, but for me, perhaps because I'm not what they call a "digital native", I just can't read things on the screen with the sustained concentration that poems require. *Tracking Wildfire* also undermines the possibility of concentration by its linkedness, so you're always zapping in and out of the document.

ST: I don't mind that but I wind up just going through the whole lot of links together, I probably don't often take advantage of that more discontinuous experience. That's maybe just because of the way I read, or at least I compel it to be all linear ultimately, despite the way it offers itself! The issue that I was interested in that linked those two books was this idea of obscurity/difficulty and transformation, which is something that came up earlier, but also what's a more obvious counter to that in *Tracking Wildfire*, being illumination.

I was focusing on 'Frog Lab' in *Embrace* because there's that statement: "to make things difficult is to make the prospect of / transformation bright and perfect".[37] It occurs quite early in the poem and obviously what follows qualifies it and alters its impact in various ways and the conclusion of the poem winds up in quite a different place. I've written "quite a lucid negotiation of the perils of writing" in my notes, although I read it again this morning and actually thought more about pregnancy!

AB: Yeah, that's right. And the loss of the idea of the child. I think there are two sets of answers. There's a more general answer about what kind of a resistance difficulty is, and that would be a question about this body of poetry in general, all of the poetry that's coming out of this particular community. And in the lines that you quote I think there is also an endorsement of an Adorno-ite vision of transformation, as well as its ironisation—which is a very Adorno-ite sort of manoeuvre—that to be bright and perfect is also to be shiny and superior and also unreal. [**ST**: It is quite loaded.]

Tracking Wildfire was really an attempt to focus on these issues much more specifically, and to think about how metaphors of illumination, of brightness and enlightenment connect the ethereal world of intellectual and artistic endeavour with a much more violent and tortured history of incendiary devices. Connecting Platonic fury, which is imagined as a flame or a fire which threatens to consume the artistic persona, to Greek fire as

---

[37] Brady, *Embrace*, p. 8.

this mysterious weapon which allows the overthrow of empires and yet nobody really knows quite what was in it, a fire which burns and sticks and cannot be put out with any water. So that felt to me like a really rich metaphoric matrix for thinking about, well, really for questioning the way that we use these terms in order to analyse or decorate our own practices—a means of showing their long history and also again of inscribing this poetic activity into the kind of material and political context which makes it possible.

To have illumination, first you need obscurity. Even God needed that! Obscurity for some poetic systems is actually an end in itself, a desideratum that the poetry is trying to achieve and yet it's also the thing which—and you picked up on this in Peter Riley's essay—separates our labour off from other kinds of human labour and ordinary human discourse. We call it ordinary in scare quotes, a "non-special speech", we'll call it that, the anthropological term "special speech" can be quite useful. So obscurity is that which cloaks our intentions and our labour, maybe by ritualizing it. I was interested in White Phosphorous as something which does both things: it illuminates—it's used on tracer fire to show where the enemy is, to illuminate the battlefield, but it's also a smokescreen and it has a capacity to produce more smoke for smaller masses of the element than most other similar products. I was thinking too about Aeneas smuggled into Carthage in a cloud provided by Venus, and troops smuggling themselves in under similar clouds, so drawing together elements of avant-garde literary practice with the actual military forward units. So that was the field of references that the poem was trying to work through. And of course, White Phosphorous is a weapon that's still being used very frequently in urban warfare, and at the time of the writing of the poem had been used very disastrously in Fallujah and has since been used in the most recent bombing in the Gaza strip.

ST: That's helpful. I was drawn to the way the poem was taking those questions on when it asks: "is obscurity / a moral option now?"[38] and the line "have I scored a blinder, or run blind / myself",[39] the way the process is raising questions about its own efficacy. You've said publicly, in the interview with Andrew Duncan, that you feel ambivalent about the piece, maybe that's superseded in a sense that you see it now as something that

---

[38] Brady, *Wildfire*, p. 56.
[39] Ibid., p. 51.

you still want to publish in another form. When you describe it as a verse-essay, what does that mean for how it's asking to be read?

AB: Well, that's a good question and in a way one that I'd like to leave up to readers. In a sense it's an attempt to remind people that the capacities of verse historically and formally have extended beyond the occasionality of the lyric that we talked about earlier. There is an attempt to unveil the sources of the poem, in part because I didn't want anyone to feel that in order to understand all the allusions that they had to replicate my labour in the libraries, but also because it's a poem which is meant to make some quite specific points and unveil some quite specific facts about the historical record and about contemporary war. The urgency that I felt about the transmission of those facts superseded my fetishisation of a kind of complex and obscure linguistic process.

Yes, we can tell our students that politicians often have recourse to metaphor and that as students of language and literature this is something they're particularly alert to, but the language of politics is also extremely explicit and you often wonder whether part of the sense of disengagement of this poetry with the political world which it's critiquing is in this development of an idiolect which is too self-regarding and too fetishistic to actually communicate the bare facts, even when it's the bare facts themselves which are the most powerful. So, yeah, blindness and scoring a blinder, I think that's what I was trying to pick up there.

ST: I'm aware how sometimes what I'm asking is already anticipating future critical writing, so I'm trying to find a place in-between because these are questions I'll consider further in some way. To broaden things out a bit, how do you see the relationship between your critical activity and creative work?

AB: I deliberately chose not to work in the field of contemporary literature because I wanted to keep my own practice separate from my paid work. I think in hindsight that that was quite a good decision, otherwise I'm put in the position—which you're very familiar with—where your poetry becomes a research output. And that leads to all sorts of discomforts and strangenesses, or it can do. Seventeenth-century literature is full of the most extraordinary vividness and political acumen, it seems to me; and there are many similarities between my favourite contemporary poets and writing that I take an inspiration from in the period. I work a great deal on women's writing and also on popular writing. It's hugely illuminating to see this abundance of popular literary activity, starting from school imitation exercises straight through to mature writers and screwballs commenting on political events such as the British civil wars. You don't see that if you're just looking at the canonical work, but it is a fascinating context for that canonical work. And the enormous radicalism of the solutions to the corruption and despotism of the monarchy, is to me just incredibly inspiring; the radical religious and prophetic movements such as the Levellers and Diggers, who really envisioned the complete transformation into a communitarian model of equality and the abolition of private property. So there's a radical challenge there that I think was never subsequently taken up in English history.

So that's how my critical work on early modern literature informs my poetic practice: because it's politically inspiring, because institutionally it's a facilitator for my independence and also because I think in terms of the style and vocabulary of the writing, everyone from Shakespeare and Milton through to extremely obscure people you wouldn't have heard of, there is a kind of linguistic profusion in that period where all discourses seem to be coming together in the imaginative sphere, in a way that is probably comparable to what we're experiencing now.

ST: That links nicely to a really striking idea that you quote at the end of that 'Dying with Honour'[40] piece, from J.C. Davis on the challenges for settlement after 1646: "how to still the plurality of discourse unleashed by the unrestrained rhetorical strategies of war".[41] which seemed to speak to current issues in very interesting ways. Counter-intuitively for me, to still the plurality of discourse could lead to a more settled political state of things, but that might be problematic as well.

AB: I think the aim of my poetry and my scholarship is to excavate that plurality of discourses from the early modern period which both literary history and conservative establishments were seeking to still—in the sense of suppress or to reduce back down to zero—with repressive mechanisms for everything from the closure of the theatres and the imposition of censorship to the torture of writers. That plurality of discourses in the early modern period is also inspirational in that it offers the hope, for those of us

---

[40] Andrea Brady, 'Dying with Honour: Literary Propaganda and the Second English Civil War' in *The Journal of Military History*, vol. 70, no. 1 (Jan, 2006), 9–30.
[41] Ibid., p. 30.

working in very obscure ways in our small, not very brightly-lit, corners of British academia, that we are writing into the historical record some kinds of resistance and the envisioning of an alternative that might be excavated by future generations of readers and scholars. So even though the efficacy of our literary action in the present is probably nil, it is there as a shout against the cold rhetoric of war and acquiescence that we hear coming out of the TV every day.

I'm working on a sequence at the moment called 'Hush Money' which is about Blackwater, or Xe, as it's been renamed, and it's got sections on the Prince and the City and the Husband. The Prince looks at Erik Prince, who was the founder of Blackwater; and the City takes Gillian Rose's notion of the three cities of Athens, Jerusalem and then Auschwitz, and recasts that in terms of thinking of Holland, Michigan (which is where Erik Prince's dad came from and where he set up his business that made millions by inventing these illuminations for car visor mirrors, vanity mirrors—somehow this invention, obscure though it seems, made millions and millions of dollars—and then Erik Prince took that money and went and set up Blackwater), so the second city is the headquarters of Blackwater in Moyock, North Carolina and the third city is Abu Ghraib.

Holland is this very strange, middle-America, Victoriana, nostalgic, perfect, little small-town community, which seems to be based very much on Dutch reformed religious morals, which of course picks up elements of the European history I've been discussing. And then Moyock is a simulacrum of a city as a crash-site: they have for example a high-school there called 'R U Ready High'[42] where SWAT teams can practice taking down students whilst a soundtrack of students screaming plays over the loudspeaker! There's planes to storm, there's buildings to fill with bullets—it's a strange kind of ghost town where they're more interested in the production of ghosts. And then obviously Abu Ghraib, which is filled with ghost detainees and the living or dying result of the practice sessions in Moyock. I also read somewhere that it had been modelled architecturally on an American university, but I can't find any corroboration of that!

One of the things that really interests me and has for a long time is the plurality of discourses, or of specialised vocabularies, that come specifically out of war. If you read accounts of mercenaries and soldiers of fortune, they're written in this very bizarre, kind of macho but very idiomatic

---

[42] See James Meek, 'Hooyah!!' *London Review of Books*, vol. 29, no. 15 (August 2007), 3–5. Viewable at: http://209.85.229.132/search?q=cache:http://www.lrb.co.uk/v29/n15/meek01_.html

language that's incredibly inventive but also very strange and unsettling. I used the term "special speech" before and it's an extraordinary instance of that. So the poem tries to unpick some of that, use it and see how it fits into both poetic discourse and "normal" language. But I haven't made as much progress on that as I'd like to have done.

ST: It sounds intriguing. To turn to another of your projects, is the Archive of the Now[43] still growing?

AB: It obviously had a little hiatus for a while! I'm trying to get some money for it now to pay for some updates. I just need to update the site and then put some old recordings that I've done that I haven't had a chance to upload; once it's completely up to date then I can start thinking again about how to develop it. But I've got some institutional support now for doing that, people are helping me and will help me to get some money for it too, so hopefully it will grow. I know it's a bit Archive of the Then at the moment, but we'll get it back up to close to now anyway!

ST: I guess I feel a certain responsibility to make it more now in a sense, add new material.

AB: That's helpful, I wish everyone did that.

ST: There must be over a hundred poets now aren't there?

AB: Yeah, definitely.

ST: Has that whole experience of doing that project fed into your creative work or influenced it in any way?

AB: You know what, not really, it really hasn't. It's been an incredible privilege but in some ways also a bit of a burden to listen to a hundred and twenty poets give me a private performance of their work! Of course in some cases hearing the voicing of the work has led me to recognise new things in it that I hadn't noticed before, and I suppose I'm familiar with a wider range of poets than perhaps I had been. But I think, because there's so little interest in and emphasis on performance amongst the poets who are represented in the Archive, I mean performance in and of itself, the readings tend to be quite professional, quite clear but not necessarily interesting in and of themselves. That's my experience, you might have a

---

[43] See: www.archiveofthenow.org/

different experience. Certainly it has influenced me as a project, in that it's made me think a little bit about what the function of the poetry reading is and whether we all pay due respect to the public nature of that kind of performance. And I would say I'm at least as guilty, if not more guilty, of neglecting that than a lot of other poets, so I've tried to raise my game in public readings since I've been working on the Archive.

ST: So you set yourself more of a challenge in performing?

AB: Yeah, well there were certain things that I did which I think are nervous habits that I picked up from other poets, but which come to seem like a stern "ethic" of performance but which I hadn't really thought through. Never explain. No concessions to the listeners: they have to be informed and earnest if they are going to enjoy this reading. The most you can hope to get from hearing any poetry reading are small slips of interest and meaning and vividness that make you want to go back and read the poems, but any kind of declaration of the poem's point or its content is a betrayal of its difficulties which leads the listeners to hear only that one thing in the poem. But the more I think about it, with no information, the standard response is probably to hear nothing in the poem, rather than at least one thing! So I've been trying to say a little bit more and contextualise the poems, and also trying to choose poems that are more suited to public performance and which make themselves available to hearing in a different way, and thinking about ensuring there's a variety of register in the poems that I do read. I'm sure that feeds back into my writing as well because I want to supply that variety, or store up some of that diversity or public viability, or performance viability, when I'm writing. So I try to write poems that can do that.

ST: I recognise that trajectory from having been of that school before! But I don't know whether, like me, you find yourself in front of more diverse audiences perhaps now, through your position? It's certainly something I associate with now having a full-time lectureship where, and as a creative writing tutor as well—I do teach literature, but increasingly less so—I am in front of very, very different audiences. When *Hold* came out, I suddenly realised it was reaching more people than any of my work ever had before and people who had no background in that kind of work at all. So I even rushed together a little preface for the launch in Liverpool to hand out to people! Actually it was mostly because I had one really over the top reaction from someone, which although it was over the top, was instructive.

AB: But negative reaction?

ST: Yeah, just because the book came on in such a way, well it was a collection that covered ten years' worth of working very much within that scene.

AB: Inevitably you always feel that the one negative reaction is more truthful than a hundred positive ones that you receive, that the insult you overheard is somehow what everyone is really thinking!

ST: Yeah, it's a bad habit! I think in this case though it's made me think that with *Internal Rhyme* I want to actually build a preface into the front of it. The fact is I've had no response to *Momentum* whatsoever! I don't think it's a particularly forbidding book but it's long, maybe that doesn't help, but it's not particularly dense and the poems are all short!

AB: Yeah, longness is a problem! I think it ties into a question you have slated for later about review culture. I know that the times I've received articulated or developed criticisms from people that it's been enormously helpful for me in thinking about the direction that my poetry's going. For example when Robin Purves wrote an essay on 'Post Festen e'—it was the poem about Thanksgiving season—his critique of that poem I thought was really spot on and actually showed me complacencies in the way I'd been working and was really helpful for me in moving in a slightly different direction.[44] We really need more of that kind of critical activity I think.

ST: You made those comments, albeit some time ago, about review culture in this country and you offered the thought that actually reading poetry meant less to people than thinking about it or identifying with it in some way. I wonder whether that's sometimes even the case amongst people who are producing within the scene?

AB: I think one problem is—it's both a problem and a delight, I suppose, a negative and positive aspect of the way that the poetic community is structured—is that everyone who participates in the forums, the email discussion lists, the little magazines and small presses and so forth, seem to be poets themselves. There are very few people who "make themselves

---

[44] Robin Purves, 'American Change: A Note on Andrea Brady and the Language of Consumption', *Edinburgh Review* 114 (2004), 177–185.

known" to the poetic community in general who are just critics and not poets. I think that, as a poet and a critic, you're always looking into this immensely productive field for some corroboration of your own activities. The worst-case scenario is that it leads to a kind of tit-for-tat review culture in which everyone is very nice and anodyne because everyone wants to get similarly blushing responses to their own work.

You could say that this is a very positive thing because it shows that poetry does one of the things which it theoretically claims for itself, which is that it turns consumers into producers and enfranchises and inspires readers to become writers and to develop their own independent productive relation to poetic language. But as a consequence there is also an enormous amount of publication and activity out there and it can become really overwhelming. If you were to try to read all the books listed as "received" on Ron Silliman's blog for example, you would just have no life whatsoever! So how do you get a handle on all that stuff? I think that the way people do get a handle on it often is to form little sodalities, reading circles and allegiances, and that's fine, but it can also lead to accusations of tribalism and the formation of non-entities like the "Cambridge School" we were discussing earlier.

ST: It's almost like because you're in that milieu and you've got one or two people responding positively because you're reading to them or you're programming them, it's maybe enough and you don't do anymore because you can't do anymore. I try and review at least one book a year, and sometimes I save them up, so I've done about six since I've been on sabbatical! Not because I'm six years behind, but I don't feel like I've done any for ages.

AB: That's good. Maybe we should have a membership committee that says you can only join the poetic community if you commit yourself to writing one review a year!

ST: Well, it would help, it would be something at least! If it was everybody who was writing and publishing it would be amazing.

AB: I think community comes up with your question about John Wilkinson, Wieners and Prynne and influences on my writing. One thing I would like to say, putting aside the influence of Wilkinson and Prynne on me for a moment, is that I very much think about my work as being produced within a community of readers and respondents. Often the responses take the form of quite informal conversations at the dinner table over a few bottles of wine! But, in addition to the high-minded influences that I cited before from the seventeenth century, I'd have to say that the work of my contemporaries has been enormously important for me in the evolution of my work, both in collaboration and competition and in difference and in admiration. Obviously, because of our personal relationship and because of our publishing together but also because of the extraordinary nature of his work, Keston Sutherland's poetry has been an absolutely formative influence on the whole of my poetry, the whole of my poetic life. And other poets that we've published through Barque like Chris Goode and Peter Manson, may be doing things which are quite different from what I'm doing but they're people for whom I have real admiration. There's a special kind of poetry that when you read it inspires a particular kind of envy, like I really wish I had written that! It's not just admiration but it's also a feeling of acquisitive desire!

The field of contemporaries whose work I've really followed would also include lots of American and Canadian writers, including Lisa Robertson, Anselm Berrigan, Kaia Sand and Jules Boykoff, Cathy Wagner, Brian Kim Stefans and Miles Champion (if he counts as American now, then I guess I count as British!). I could go on. But one thing that's really exciting now is that a lot of the old concerns that we had about gender and the under-representation of women within what you are calling the innovative poetry community [**ST**: Don't pin it on me!] have receded. In this new generation there are lots of exciting women writers.

ST: Yes, it's getting a lot better.

AB: So, having said that, it's nice to have the opportunity to address the relation of my work to Prynne's and Wilkinson's. Obviously I've written on both of them before and I'm very engaged with them as friends. We've published their books and Wilkinson at least has written about me. I have a lot of admiration for them both as writers and as people. Wilkinson is another poet about whom I feel this kind of acquisitive envy. There are aspects of his linguistic imagination which I think are totally unique—nobody has quite the facility of invention that he has. He writes enormous quantities of verse and it's all really excellent and within it you really have what feels like the whole of the built environment and the whole of human trade. Every object seems to have found its way into John's poetry at one point or another, and I'm immensely jealous and awestruck by that. It's interesting to see what's happening to his poetry in the ways that it's opening up, now that he's in the States and perhaps engaging in this different kind of conversational field and linguistic usage. He's gone in the opposite geographical direction from the one I took in my 20's! And so his poetry in *Down to Earth*[45] and so forth is becoming more accessible and more forthright and clear and that's been noted by several reviewers.

One reservation I have about his work is that syntactically it is quite static. There is a grammatical structure that he prefers which is: an inanimate object, an active verb—often a transitive verb—in present tense and then its object. And that might seem like a minor thing, and just a stylistic tic, but it's one that is repeated pervasively in work from round that time of *Contrivances*[46] through to the present. In *Down to Earth* there may be more of a presence of a lyric "I" if we'd like to call it that, but I think that this way of working, this syntactic structure, exaggerates the impression that John subscribes to a "postmodern" view of the place of the subject which I was mentioning earlier: that the user has been extracted from networks of interference and the chain of action and reaction persists only amongst the objects. It's almost as if you're living in a universe taken over by nanotechnology, a mechanised universe where all objects are animated and all acting on each other. There are forces and flows of energy between them, which is a way of showing that human agency has been suppressed and sequestered, but it's also a distortion of relations and activity, pointing it all entirely towards the present, towards the materiality of the present condition. Interestingly there's very little reflection on the past in John's work. And that's one big difference between us, I would say: that there's no archaeology for Wilkinson.

ST: Which is actually a similar argument to what you're proposing about Wieners' work in that piece on *Jacket*,[47] you focus on his writing on presentness.

AB: Maybe that has something to do with where it's coming from for John. It's almost as if his energy is so consumed in the representation of

---

[45] John Wilkinson, *Down to Earth* (Great Wilbraham: Salt Publishing, 2008).
[46] John Wilkinson, *Contrivances* (Great Wilbraham: Salt Publishing, 2003).
[47] Andrea Brady, 'The Other Poet: John Wieners, Frank O'Hara, and Charles Olson', originally published in *Don't Ever Get Famous: Essays on New York Writing after the New York School*, ed. Daniel Kane (Champaign, IL: Dalkey Archive Press, 2006), pp. 317–347.

this over-populated, mechanised, animatronic universe, that's there's not as much of a sense of reflection on past difference and, for that reason, future determinations (I daren't say self-determinations). Maybe that's over-theorising what is essentially a stylistic tic, but it's one way which I would distinguish my work from John's.

ST: I keep mentioning John today, but I'm just as aware of the differences in your practices as the similarities. His work is just one of the things I'm using to think through the broader field of where you fit in and where I fit in and where everybody is situated.

AB: I think it's helpful to define yourself in opposition to and in admiration of another poet: not just because it helps you to learn new techniques, but also because it helps you to articulate what you want your poetry to be and do. That would be true too of Jeremy Prynne. My feelings about Prynne's work are much more complicated in a way and my admiration is much more dampened in some ways. Prynne has been extraordinarily influential for me and for most people I know, and not just as a poet but also as a teacher, and as someone who is protective and interventionist and helpful in this community and limitlessly generous and good to talk to. Emotionally he has been incredibly available to many of my friends, women and men, and he can be just amazingly kind. However, I see his recent work as reaching towards an apogee which goes far beyond a limit that I would want to set for negativity and resistance. There is a vicious tensility of the late work which allows nothing to escape; there is no opportunity in it for freedom, or self-determination, or happiness, or kindness, or intimacy.

Prynne often talks about his works in terms of a dialectic and in his essay in *Quid* 6 on Handke's dictum about war and language from 2000,[48] he alludes to Eliot's remark about purifying the language of the tribe and says that language is the tribal memory that includes the best and the worst, the most noble and most vicious aspects of human history. I think that essay was perhaps the last moment when he was willing to endorse the idea that there could any nobility in language. I side with him in this belief that you can't have the best without also taking the worst, and that view has inspired a lot of my work, but more recent collections have just continuously narrowed down the possibility for meaning-making

---

[48] J. H. Prynne, 'A Quick Riposte to Handke's Dictum about War and Language' in *Quid* 6 (2000), 23–26. Viewable at: http://www.barquepress.com/quid6.pdf

and meaning-endorsement and freedom of any kind. Yes, they reveal how entrapped we are in the languages of war and of capital, but they're also themselves disturbingly tyrannical. There's very little that I can make of them. I don't experience any sense of freedom or liberation when I'm reading them. It's not just that I don't get to participate as a reader in making meaning or anything like that. There's no creativity allowed to me as a reader, there's no room for it, but they are also absolutely rebarbative of understanding. I'm not just complaining that I can't understand them, I hope! But that the poems themselves whittle down more and more the possibility of understanding. Ironically, even though they are full of these extraordinarily dense and inclusive references to every kind of human knowledge, reading them is in a funny way actually an experience of antiknowledge.

That's part of the difficulty I have with *To Pollen*,[49] which is something I've wanted to address formally for a long time, and hopefully I'll get a chance to write on it at some point, but there is for me an extremely problematic moment in that sequence where he talks about an image that might be from the bombing of Qana or it might be from any footage you can see on Al-Jazeera, of a man cradling the body of his dead son. It comes at a point where the poem has so corrupted the idea of representation and the abuses of language that it can only be emblematic of how such imagery is used and distorted for media consumption and the pathos of our own ideas of political subjectivity. But to my mind that instrumentalises that suffering for the theoretical purpose of aesthetic- and ideology-critique, quite as effectively as its broadcast might have done.

ST: So that would be almost the Adorno moment of autonomous art nevertheless exploiting suffering for its own ends?

AB: Yeah, but without any sense, as there is in Adorno, that poetry can represent this kind of glimmer of a different future.

ST: Is 'Refuse Collection' in that book?

AB: No, I don't think 'Refuse Collection' is collected! It's in *IRA Quid*.[50] It's not been published anywhere else since then.

---

[49] J. H. Prynne, *To Pollen* (London and Brighton: Barque Press, 2006).
[50] J.H. Prynne, 'Refuse Collection', *Ira Quid* 13 (2004). Viewable at: http://www.barquepress.com/quid13.html

ST: I've just been reading an essay for the journal about it and the author raises similar issues with that text.[51]

AB: It's almost as if Prynne, whose personality is very oppositional, has so devoutly eschewed the transcendental ideas about language that he had in his earliest work, that he's now nailed to the negative image of them. There's something as transcendental about that absolute squashing of any potentiality for hope or communication or kindness or beauty in the late work, as there was in the hope that in language there was some possibility for self-identity that was present in the early work. I just don't go along with that. I think that is to cut out, and perhaps here I am sounding a bit like Peter Riley, the realities of personal happiness that all of us, even the most downtrodden and exploited person, experience. So that's my line on Prynne!

ST: John actually raises similar, but qualified, issues about *Embrace* in *The Lyric Touch*.[52] I have no doubts about the fact that your work does admit those possibilities and I think the more I've reflected on the idea that possibility is the best we can get, the more I'm comfortable with it. However, I'm still wanting there to be those actual actualities, as well as possibilities! But certainly the kinds of things you're describing about your experiences of reading Prynne are ones I recognise. I've had very empowering experiences of the early work, and I try to keep abreast of his development, but it has gone into a very intractable position lately.

AB: He talks about no valorisation of process, in the letter to Steve McCaffery, no free lunch, I forget what the quote is exactly, he's talking about how choices in poetry are illusory and it's just replicating the structure of false choice which is available to anyone in a western supermarket.[53] It's

---

[51] See Ian Davidson, 'Democratic Consensus in J.H. Prynne's "Refuse Collection"', *Journal of British and Irish Innovative Poetry*, vol. 1, no. 1 (September 2009), 37–53.
[52] See John Wilkinson, 'Off the Grid: Lyric and Politics in Andrea Brady's *Embrace*' in Wilkinson's *The Lyric Touch* (Great Wilbraham: Salt Publishing, 2007), pp. 120–139.
[53] "Consumption, to be renamed as production: the *open* text, the *inventive*, *selective* reader, free to opt for useful waste or wasteful utility. [...] Isn't the supermarket the correct analogy, where the consumer is generically trained to value a freedom of choice precisely fetishised by the brand alternatives of late capitalism[?]" J.H. Prynne, 'A Letter to Steve McCaffery', *The Gig* 7 (November 2000), 40–46, p. 41.

almost as if, in order to counter that illusion of free choice in poetry which is just an extension of the freedom of the Western consumer, the later work allows the reader no choice at all. But the texts themselves feel in some ways also encumbered by their superfluity, the superfluity and surplus of the language. It's as if we're being taken into the word-supermarket and shown lots of strange objects on the shelves which we can't buy or use, just to make us feel that frustration, for the first time in our lives, of not being able to have something. Or like a chained library!

But on the other hand, I don't believe that they are intended to be abstract conceptual works, in which all of the materials are there and if you were to remix them you could make your own nice little bit of anti-art. But nonetheless, the experience for me is just one of real imprisonment in the text as a reader, I can't make anything out of it.

That's his particular personal trajectory and it's quite cognizable in the pattern that it's taken, but I don't think it's a model that should be followed religiously! There are a lot of younger poets who have been very influenced by Prynne's late style and are echoing aspects of it, but not having passed through the same personal and ethical dilemmas that he's gone through. Such poetry risks ending up with a kind of junk-heap of words in a way.

ST: I was discussing this problem with Caroline about how important it is, when one is a teacher of creative writing wanting to introduce students to this work, to give a sense of theoretical background, historical context, to give those motivations. Because otherwise the techniques can be grasped enormously quickly and put to use to make things which are effectively simulations of the work, but with enough superficial dazzle to convince a younger writer that they've achieved something. Maybe that's also nevertheless a process that one has to go through as a younger writer, to imitate until one realises the limits of imitation.

AB: Yeah, you start off filled with excitement about these strange poems and even though you may not really understand them you can see how their techniques expand your own capacities. And then someone forces you to analyse and critique them and takes all the joy out of your life. Maybe we sound like the UN trying to control Iran's nuclear enrichment programme! First you must learn … but in the wrong hands these techniques are very dangerous! But I do worry about a trend towards obscurity, towards diffusion and confusion in contemporary poetry. I think that it can also be a way of masking insecurities, particularly in younger writers, and I myself have been susceptible to this in the past, of masking insecurities about what you know or don't know or are doing by offering and withholding communication simultaneously. I'm certainly not flying the flag for clarity and sincerity in poetry, but also I think we need to be very careful not to be scornful of our readers, and treat any kind of transfer of thought or feeling as somehow a weakness or a concession to the laziness of the consumer under late capitalism.

Peter Manson is someone who, I think, achieves this balance between communication and difficulty, clarity and exquisite materialities of language, very effectively. Keston is another. I think people who want to align Keston's work with Jeremy's—obviously the two are very connected because of Keston's PhD thesis and because they're so close as friends—make an error because I think that what Keston's doing now is actually something entirely different, using the burlesque and the bathetic in order to engage his audience. His ludicrous stories and closet dramas are actually not hugely difficult to follow, and they're even sometimes pleasurable! Oh God, now I sound like Kenneth Koch. For example, in 'Stress Position',[54] the poem that he's working on now, the early sexual life of Black Beauty is conflated with a suicide bombing in a McDonald's in Baghdad! And it's funny! But the motility of the small fragments and bits of language detritus that he uses do not contribute to a sense of overpowering obscurity. They feel much more like part of the compositional structure: they're not there to intercede between you and the meaning, they're part of the architectural frame of the poem, and sonically they make a certain kind of sense—they're entertaining and interesting and rich in the mouth and on the ear. So that's something that feels to me quite different to what Prynne has ended up with. The most recent book, *Streak Willing Entourage Artesian*,[55] I find very difficult, very rebarbative, and as I said, almost tyrannical.

ST: Have you published that?

AB: Yeah, we have! [laughter] I have to say, as much as I admire Prynne and I know that people are right when they say that he is one of the most significant poets of the twentieth and now the twenty-first century, that book is also for me a dead end.

---

[54] Keston Sutherland, *Stress Position* (London and Brighton: Barque Press, 2009).
[55] J.H. Prynne, *Streak Willing Entourage Artesian* (London and Brighton: Barque Press, 2009).

Bibliographies

KAREN MAC CORMACK

Books
Tale Light: New and Selected Poems 1984–2009 (Toronto/Sheffield: Book Thug/ West House Books, 2010)
Implexures (Complete Edition), (Tucson/Sheffield: Chax Press/West House, 2008)
Implexures (Vol. 1), (Tucson, AZ/Sheffield: Chax Press/West House Books, 2003)
Vanity Release (La Laguna, Tenerife: Zasterle Press, 2003)
At Issue (Toronto: Coach House Books, 2001)
Fit To Print (with Alan Halsey), (Toronto/Sheffield: Coach House Books/West House Books, 1998)
The Tongue Moves Talk (Tucson, AZ, Hay-on-Wye: Chax Press/West House Books, 1997)
Marine Snow (Toronto: ECW Press, 1995)
Quirks & Quillets (Tucson, AZ: Chax Press, 1991)
Quill Driver (London: Nightwood Editions, 1989)
Straw Cupid (Toronto: Nightwood Editions, 1987)

Chapbooks and Broadsides
Plural Modifiers (broadside), (Sheffield: Gargoyle Editions, 2006)
Nothing By Mouth (reprint), (Toronto: Book Thug, 2003)
From a Middle (with Steve McCaffery), (Calgary: Housepress, 2002)
PALM (broadside), (Buffalo, NY: Buffalo Broadsides No. 9, 2001)
from Implexures (Calgary: Housepress, 2001)
Multiplex (with Ron Silliman), (Bray: Wild Honey Press, 1998)
Nothing by Mouth (Toronto: Underwhich Editions, 1984)

Anthologies
PULLLLLLLLLLL: Poesia Contemporânea do Canadá, eds. John Havelda, Isabel Patim & Manuel Portela (Lisbon: Antígona Editores Refractários, 2010)
Prismatic Publics: Innovative Canadian Women's Poetry and Poetics, eds. Kate Eichorn and Heather Milne (Toronto: Coach House Books, 2009)
Another Language: Poetic Experiments in Britain and North America, eds. Kornelia Freitag and Katharina Vester (Münster: LIT Verlag, 2008)
Audiatur (Katalog for Ny Poesi), (Bergen: Norsk Forfattersentrum, 2005)
Vectors: New Poetics, ed. Robert Archambeau (Lincoln, NE: Samizdat Editions, 2001)
Poesia do Mondo 3, (Porto: Edições Afrontamento, 2001)
POGONE (Tucson: POG and Chax Press, 1999)
Moving Borders: Three Decades of Innovative Writing by Women, ed. Mary Margaret Sloan (Jersey City, NJ: Talisman House, 1998)

Introduction

Coach House Books Y2OK (Toronto: Coach House Books, 1998)
Carnival: a Scream in High Park reader, ed. Peter McPhee (Toronto: Insomniac Press, 1996)
Out of Everywhere: Linguistically Innovative Poetry by Women in North America & the UK, ed. Maggie O'Sullivan (London: Reality Street Editions, 1996)
The Gertrude Stein Awards in Innovative North American Poetry: 1993–1994, ed. Douglas Messerli (Los Angeles: Sun & Moon Press, 1995)
The Last Word, ed. Michael Holmes (Toronto: Insomniac Press, 1995)
The Art of Practice: Forty-five Contemporary Poets, eds. Peter Ganick, Dennis Barone (Elmwood, CT: Potes & Poets Press, 1994)
Into the Nightlife, eds. David Lee, Maureen Cochrane (Toronto: Nightwood Editions, 1986)

Critical Work

'Self-Amusement', in *Formes Poétiques Contemporaines* 8 (June 2011), 109–113
'Effet de cygnificants: le pli et la pratique interdisciplinaire', in *Le Rossignol Instrumental: Poésie, Musique, Modernité*, eds. Jean-Pierre Bertrand, Michel Delville, Christine Pagnoulle, tr. Piotr Burzykowski (Leuven, Paris & Dudley, MA: Peeters Vrin, 2004), 139–150
'Mutual Labyrinth: a proposal of exchange', in *Architectures of Poetry*, eds. María Eugenia Díaz Sánchez, Craig Douglas Dworkin (Amsterdam & New York: Rodopi, 2004), 109–116

Recordings

Double Change no. 2 – A film archive of poetry: 2005–2006 (reading with Bernard Heidsieck and Steve McCaffery, Place Ephémere, Paris 2006) (Dijon: Le Presses du Réel, 2009) (1 hour 20 min DVD)
Another Language: Contemporary US-American Poetic Experiment in a Changing World (reading with Steve McCaffery, Rühr Universität), curated by Jelle Dierickx (Ghent University: b*bobeobi*archive05, 2005) (1 hour CD)
New Writing Series (interview and reading), curated by Steve Evans (Orono, ME: University of Maine, 2004) (30 min video)
Nothing By Mouth film (1984, director Annette Mangaard) based on three poems in *Nothing By Mouth* converted to DVD with new Mac Cormack voice-over and new music composed and recorded by Keir Brownstone, 2004.
LINEbreak (Interviews and performance), Charles Bernstein (Interviewer/Co-producer), Martin Spinelli (Producer/ Director). (WBFO 88.7 NPR News & Jazz, 1996) (30 min audio cassette)
Quill Driver (London & Ontario: Nightwood Editions, 1989) (40 min audio cassette)

Online Resources
Author page at the Electronic Poetry Center (State University of New York at Buffalo): http://wings.buffalo.edu/epc/authors/maccormack
Author page at Penn Sound: http://writing.upenn.edu/pennsound/x/MacCormack.php
PhillyTalks 19 (pre-event correspondence with Allen Fisher), at: http://slought.org/files/downloads/domains/phillytalks/pdf/pt19.pdf.
PhillyTalks 19 (recording of event on Penn Sound), at:
http://www.writing.upenn.edu/pennsound/phillytalks/Philly-Talks-Episode19.html

JENNIFER MOXLEY

Books
There Are Things We Live Among: Essays on the Object World (Chicago: Flood Editions, forthcoming 2012)
Clampdown (Chicago: Flood Editions, 2009)
The Middle Room (Berkeley, CA: Subpress, 2007)
The Line (Sausalito, CA: The Post-Apollo Press, 2007)
Often Capital (Chicago: Flood Editions, 2005)
The Sense Record (Washington, DC: Edge Books, 2002). Reprinted Great Wilbraham: Salt Publishing, 2003
Imagination Verses (New York: Tender Buttons, 1996). Reprinted Great Wilbraham: Salt Publishing, 2003
Evidence des Lumières (Trans. of *Enlightenment Evidence* (see below) (Grâne: Editions Créaphis, 1998)

Chapbooks and Broadsides
Evacuations (Northampton, MA: Least Weasel Press, forthcoming 2012)
Coastal (Amherst, MA: The Song Cave, 2011)
'Lost Solitary Meanings' (broadside) (Boston: Arrowsmith Press, 2007)
Fragments of a Broken Poetics (Orono, ME: Impercipient Editions, 2006)
The Occasion (New York: Belladonna, 2002)
Wrong Life (Cambridge: Equipage, 1999)
Enlightenment Evidence (Cambridge: rem press, 1996)
Ten Still Petals (Providence: privately published, 1996)
The First Division of Labour (Boston: Rosetta Chapbook, 1995)

Translations
Anne Portugal, *Absolute bob* (Providence, RI: Burning Deck, 2010)

Jacqueline Risset, from *Jeu*, in *Talisman Anthology of Francophone Poetry*, ed. Kristin Prevallet et al (Jersey City, NJ: Talisman House, forthcoming).

Madeleine Gagnon, from *Chant pour une Québec lontaine*, in *Talisman Anthology of Francophone Poetry*, ed. Kristin Prevallet et al (Jersey City, NJ: Talisman House, forthcoming).

Jacqueline Risset, *Sleep's Powers* (New York: Ugly Duckling Presse, 2008)

Jacqueline Risset, *The Translation Begins* (Providence, RI: Burning Deck, 1996)

Anthologies

American Hybrid: A Norton Anthology of New Poetry (New York: Norton, 2009)

Vanishing Points: New Modernist Poems, eds. Rod Mengham and John Kinsella (Great Wilbraham: Salt Publishing, 2004)

Isn't It Romantic: 100 Love Poems by Younger American Poets, eds. Brett Fletcher Lauer and Aimee Kelley (Seattle, WA: Verse Press, 2004)

The Best American Poetry, ed. Robert Creeley (New York: Scribner, 2002).

The Mechanics of the Mirage: Postwar American Poetry, eds. Michel Delville and Christine Pagnoulle (Liège: Université de Liège: 2000)

An Anthology of New (American) Poets, eds. Lisa Jarnot, Christopher Stroffolino, and Leonard Schwartz (Jersey City, NJ: Talisman House, 1998)

Editorial Work

Contributing editor of *The Poker* since 2003

Poetry editor of *The Baffler* 1997–2010

Co-editor of *The Impercipient Lecture Series* (10 issues in 1997)

Editor of *The Impercipient* 1992–1995. See online archive at *Arras*.

Critical Work (selection)

'Dérive-ations: Pierre Joris & the Drift of Tradition', in *Pierre Joris: Cartographies of the In-Between*, ed. Peter Cockelbergh (Prague: Litteraria Pragensia Books, 2011)

'On Writing *The Middle Room*', *Esopus* 13 (2009)

'Jennifer Moxley on Susan Howe', in *Women Poets on Mentorship: Efforts and Affections*, eds. Areille Greenberg and Rachel Zucker (Iowa City: University of Iowa Press, 2008)

'Subject and Matter: Interview with Fanny Howe', *The Modern Review*, vol. 2, no. 3 (2007)

'Rimbaud's Foolish Virgin, Wieners's "Feminine Soliloquy" and the Metaphorical Resistance of the Lyric Body', *Talisman* 34 (2007). Reprinted online in *Jacket* 34 (2007)

'Lyric Poetry and the Inassimilable Life', *The Poker* 6 (2005)

'Notes on Politics, Form, & Experiment', *Review of Two Worlds: French and*

American Poetry in Translation, ed. Béatrice Mousli (Los Angeles: Otis Books/Seismicity Editions, 2005)
'Ancients and Contemporaries', *The Poker* 2 (2003)
From 'The Language Albatross – Autobiographical Writings', *The Paper* 5 (Oct 2002)
'A Personal Reminiscence Chronicling the First Documented Case of "The Waldrop Effect"', *How2*, vol. 1, no. 8 (Fall 2002)
'Innovative Poetry after Language Poetry', *OEI* 7–8 (2001)
'The Sphere of Generality – On Content', *Open Letter*, vol. 11, no. 3 (2001)
'Editing and Gender: *The Impercipient*', *Chain* 1 (1994). Reprinted online at *Arras*.
'Invective Verse', *Oblek* 12: *Writing from the New Coast* (1993)

Online Resources
Author page at the Electronic Poetry Center (State University of New York at Buffalo): http://epc.buffalo.edu/authors/moxley/
Author page at Penn Sound: http://writing.upenn.edu/pennsound/x/Moxley.php

CAROLINE BERGVALL

Performances / Installations (selection)
Middling English, John Hansard Gallery, Southampton, September–October 2010
Say: 'Parsley', Arnolfini Gallery, Bristol, 8 May–4 July 2010
Say: 'Parsley', MuKha, Museum of Contemporary Arts, Antwerp, 23 May–6 August 2008
Little Sugar (iivv) (text-sound installation collaboration), Text Festival Commission, Bury, 2005
Say: 'Parsley', Liverpool Biennial, November 2004
DOG (public text), *LLAW & BookArtBookshop*, Pitfield Street, London, October 2002
Say: 'Parsley', Spacex Gallery, Exeter, 18–29 November 2001
ECLAT – sites 1–10. Commissioned by the Institution of Rot (London) for Literature Live (LAB), May 1996
Strange Passage (choral poem). Awarded Live Art Commission, The Showroom Gallery London, 1993

Introduction

Books
Meddle English (New York: Nightboat, 2011)
Middling English, catalogue with CD (Southampton: John Hansard Publications, 2011)
Plessjør (Oslo: H-Press, 2008)
Fig (Goan Atom 2), (Great Wilbraham: Salt Publishing, 2005)
ÉCLAT, online pdf edition (New York: Ubu Editions, 2004)
Goan Atom: 1.Doll (San Francisco: Kruspkaya Books, 2001)
ECLAT – sites 1–10 (Lowestoft: Sound & Language, 1996)

Chapbooks
Alyson Singes (New York: Belladonna Books, 2009)
Cropper (Southampton: Torque Press, 2008)
8 Figs (Cambridge: Equipage, 2004)
GONG (New York: Belladonna, 2004)
Jets-Poupee (Cambridge: rem press, 1999)
Strange Passage (Cambridge: Equipage, 1993)

Translation
Typhon Dru, texts by French-Canadian poet Nicole Brossard (London: Reality Street Editions, 1997)

Anthologies
Infinite Difference: Other Poetries by UK Women Poets, ed. Carrie Etter (Exeter: Shearsman Books, 2010)
The McSweeney's Book of Poets Picking Poets, ed. Dominic Luxford (New York: McSweeney's, 2007)
The Oxford Anthology of Modern British and Irish Poetry, ed. Keith Tuma (New York: Oxford University Press, 2001)
FLÈSH ACOEUR, artist handmade booklet, commissioned for *Volumes of Vulnerability: 20 artists/writers*, ed. Kate Meynell & Susan Johanknecht (London: Gefn Press, 2000)
Foil: Defining Poetry, 1985–2000, ed. N. Johnson (Buckfastleigh: etruscan books, 2000)
Out of Everywhere: Linguistically Innovative Poetry by Women in North America & the UK, ed. Maggie O'Sullivan (London: Reality Street, 1996)
Conductors of Chaos, ed. Iain Sinclair (London: Picador, 1996)
Language Alive 2, ed. cris cheek (London: Sound & Language, 1996)

Critical Work (selection)

'Prepositional space, site-specific work and bilingual poetics', Keynote Address, *Sexuate Subjects: Politics, Ethics, Poetics*, UCL, London, 4 December 2010 (proceeds forthcoming)

'Middling English: Nodalities of Writing', Keynote Address, *Contemporary Women's Writing: New Texts, Approaches and Technologies*, SDSU, San Diego, 7 July 2010. Reproduced in *Meddle English* (2011)

'Pressure Points: Gendered and Tactical Authorship', *How2*, vol. 3, no. 3 (Nov 2009)

'Cat in the Throat – on bilingual occupants', in *Jacket* 37 (Spring 2009); in *What we see is what we hear* arts catalogue, Henie Onstad Museet, Oslo, Norwegian translation (Summer 2009)

'Social Engagement of Writing' at Conceptual Poetry and its Others symposium, convened by Marjorie Perloff, Arizona Poetry Center, Tucson, 29–30 May 2008

'The audio culture of writing', *Kritiker* 7 (December 2007) (in English online)

'Short Aside to the Franker Tale', *Jacket* 32 (Spring 2007)

'O Yes' (with Erín Moure), *Antiphonies: Essays on Women's Experimental Poetries in Canada*, ed. Nate Dorward (Toronto: The Gig, 2007), pp. 167–76

'Georges Perec's site-writings', in *The /n/oulipean Analects* (Los Angeles: Les Figues Press, 2007)

'Stepping out with Kenneth Goldsmith: a New York interview' in *Open Letter*, vol. 12, no. 7 (Fall 2005)

'Handwriting as a Form of Protest: Fiona Templeton's *Cells of Release*', *Jacket* 26 (October 2004)

'Body & Sign: Some thoughts around the work of Aaron Williamson, Hannah Weiner, and Henri Michaux', *Jacket* 22 (May 2003)

'A form of address: Essay-Review of *A Conversation with David Antin* by David Antin & Charles Bernstein (Granary Books: NY, 2002)', *Jacket* 22 (May 2003)

'In the Place of Writing' in *Assembling Alternatives: Reading Postmodern Poetries Transnationally*, ed. Romana Huk (Middletown: Wesleyan University Press, 2003), pp. 327–337.

'Piece in Progress: About Face (*Goan Atom*, 2)', *How2*, vol. 1, no. 6 (Fall 2001)

'Writing at the Cross-roads of Languages' in *Telling it Slant: Avant-Garde Poetics of the 1990s*, eds. Steven Marks & Mark Wallace (Tuscaloosa & London: University of Alabama Press, 2001), pp. 207–223.

Recordings

Playing with Words, CD, audio compilation ed. Cathy Lane (London: Gruen 065, 2010)

'More Pets', CD, DJ Rupture, *Solar Life Raft* (New York: Agriculture, 2009)
Shorter Chaucer Tales. Launched as audiotexts on PennSound (2006)
Overheard, CD, audio compilation ed. Kenneth Goldsmith (Boston: ICA, 2006)
Via: Poems 1994–2004, CD, *Rockdrill* 8 (Optic Nerve/Birkbeck College: London, Autumn 2005)
Agents of Impurity, 2CD, ed. Kenneth Goldsmith (London: Sonic Arts Network, 2004)
Frequency, CD, ed. CA Conrad & Maggie Zurawski (Philadelphia & San Francisco, 2004)

Online Resources
Personal website: www.carolinebergvall.com
Author page at Archive of the Now: http://www.archiveofthenow.org/authors/?i=2
Author page at the Electronic Poetry Center (State University of New York at Buffalo): http://epc.buffalo.edu/authors/bergvall/
Author page at Penn Sound: http://writing.upenn.edu/pennsound/x/Bergvall.php
Author page at Poets.org: http://www.poets.org/poet.php/prmPID/2153
Author page at ubuweb: http://www.ubu.com/sound/bergvall.html

ANDREA BRADY

Books
The Rushes (Hastings: Reality Street, forthcoming 2012)
Wildfire: A Verse Essay on Obscurity and Illumination (San Francisco: Krupskaya, 2010). Original hypertext poem published on *dispatx.com* (2007)
Embrace (Glasgow: Object Permanence, 2005)
Vacation of a Lifetime (Great Wilbraham: Salt Publishing, 2001)

Chapbooks
Cold Calling (Cambridge: Barque Press, 2004)
Liberties (New York: Potes & Poets, 1999)
Cranked Foil (Cambridge: Poetical Histories, 1997)

Anthologies and Work in Translation
Infinite Difference: Other Poetries by UK Women Poets, ed. by Carrie Etter (Exeter: Shearsman Books, 2010)

Translated into Spanish for the anthology *La isla tuerta: 49 poetas británicos (1946–2006)* (Madrid: Lumen Editorial, 2009)
Poems with French translations published in *cipM 147* (Marseille, May 2006)

Critical Work (selection)
'Making Use of the Pain: the John Wieners Archives', *Paideuma* 36 (July 2010), 131–179
'Distraction and Absorption on Second Avenue', in *Frank O'Hara Now: New Essays on the New York Poet*, eds. Will Montgomery and Robert Hampson (Liverpool: Liverpool University Press, February 2010), pp. 59–69
'Letter to Bob Archambeau', *Cambridge Literary Review* 2 (January 2010), 244–249
'Shadowy Figures in *Quill, Solitary Apparition* by Barbara Guest', *Chicago Review*, vol. 53, no. 4 and vol. 54, no. 1/2 (2008), 120–125
'On Poetry and Public Pleasure: a reading of Tom Raworth', in *Poetry and Public Language*, ed. Tony Lopez (Exeter: Shearsman Books, 2007), pp. 25–36
'The Other Poet: John Wieners, Frank O'Hara, and Charles Olson' in *Don't Ever Get Famous: Essays on New York Writing after the New York School*, ed. Daniel Kane (Illinois State University: Dalkey Archive Press, Dec. 2006), pp. 317–347. Reprinted on *Jacket* 32 (April 2007)
'Zero Longitude: Notes on Kevin Nolan's Elegiac Centres', *The Paper* 5 (Oct 2002), 27–35; reprinted in *Necessary Steps: Poetry, Elegy, Walking, Spirit*, ed. David Kennedy (Exeter: Shearsman Books, 2007), pp. 11–27
'No Turning Back: *Acrylic Tips*', *Quid 17: for J. H. Prynne, in Celebration* (24 June 2006), 80–83
'For Immediate Delivery: on the semiotics of blogs' in *Put About: a critical anthology on independent publishing*, ed. Maria Fusco and Ian Hunt (London: Book Works, 2004), pp. 139–147
'Grief Work in a War Economy', *Radical Philosophy* 114 (July/Aug, 2002), 7–12

Review Articles
'The Same War Continues: Denise Levertov, *New Selected Poems*', *Poetry Review*, vol. 94, no. 2 (2004), 76–8
'Object Lessons: George Oppen, *New Collected Poems*', *Poetry Review*, vol. 94, no. 1 (2004), 64–70
'Walking and Standing Still in Suffolk: RF Langley, *More or Less*', *Poetry Review*, vol. 93, no. 1 (2003), 67–73
'Out of This World: Peter Robinson, *Poetry, Poets, Readers: Making Things Happen*', *Poetry Review*, vol. 92, no. 4 (Winter 2002), 96–99
'The Middle Distance: Lorine Niedecker, *Collected Poems*', *Poetry Review*, vol. 92, no. 3 (2002), 87–91

Introduction

Review of *Left Under a Cloud* by Stephen Rodefer, *Jacket* 15 (Dec 2001)
'Brief Notes on *Reverses* by John Wilkinson', *Jacket* 9 (Oct 1999)

Online Resources
Staff page at University of London: http://www.english.qmul.ac.uk/staff/bradya.html

www.ingramcontent.com/pod-product-compliance
Lightning Source LLC
Chambersburg PA
CBHW022013160426
43197CB00007B/406